EASY GUITAR
WITH NOTES & TAB

CHART HITS OF 2019 2020

ISBN 978-1-5400-8549-8

HAL•LEONARD®

Visit Hal Leonard Online at
www.halleonard.com

Contact us:
Hal Leonard
7777 West Bluemound Road
Milwaukee, WI 53213
Email: info@halleonard.com

In Europe, contact:
Hal Leonard Europe Limited
42 Wigmore Street
Marylebone, London, W1U 2RN
Email: info@halleonardeurope.com

In Australia, contact:
Hal Leonard Australia Pty. Ltd.
4 Lentara Court
Cheltenham, Victoria, 3192 Australia
Email: info@halleonard.com.au

STRUM AND PICK PATTERNS

This chart contains the suggested strum and pick patterns that are referred to by number at the beginning of each song in this book. The symbols ⊓ and ∨ in the strum patterns refer to down and up strokes, respectively. The letters in the pick patterns indicate which right-hand fingers play which strings.

p = thumb
i = index finger
m = middle finger
a = ring finger

For example; Pick Pattern 2
is played: thumb - index - middle - ring

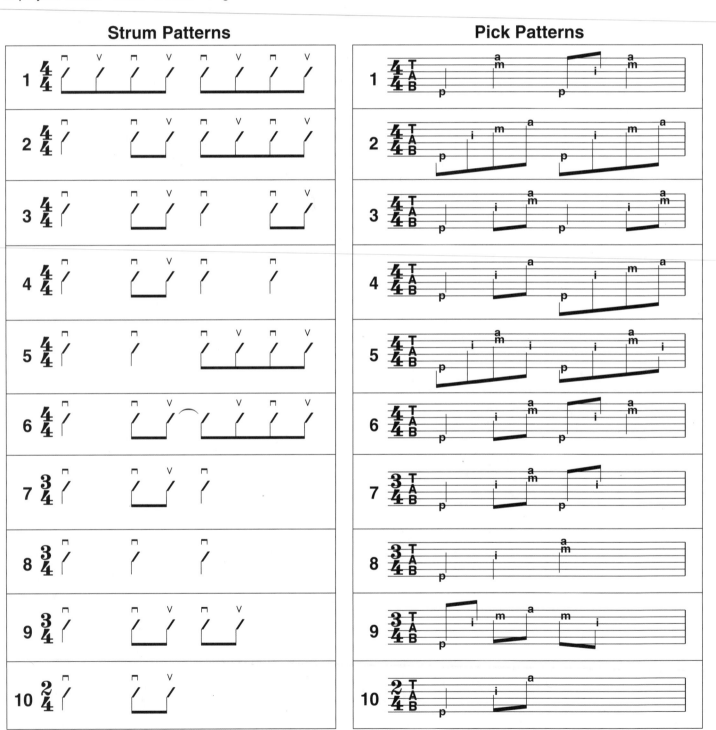

You can use the 3/4 Strum and Pick Patterns in songs written in compound meter (6/8, 9/8, 12/8, etc.). For example, you can accompany a song in 6/8 by playing the 3/4 pattern twice in each measure. The 4/4 Strum and Pick Patterns can be used for songs written in cut time (¢) by doubling the note time values in the patterns. Each pattern would therefore last two measures in cut time.

Beautiful People

Words and Music by Ed Sheeran, Khalid Robinson, Fred Gibson, Max Martin and Shellback

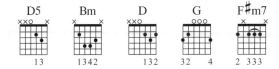

*Capo I

Strum Pattern: 1
Pick Pattern: 1

Intro
Moderately slow, in 2

(We are, ___ we are, ___ we are.) ___

*Optional: To match recording, place capo at 1st fret.

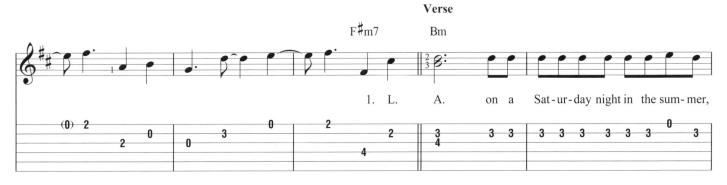

Verse

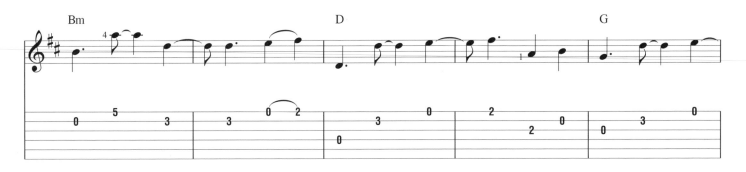

1. L. A. on a Sat-ur-day night in the sum-mer,

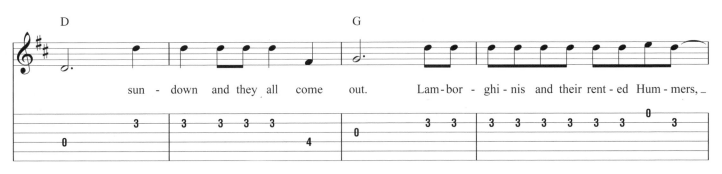

sun - down and they all come out. Lam-bor - ghi - nis and their rent-ed Hum-mers, ___

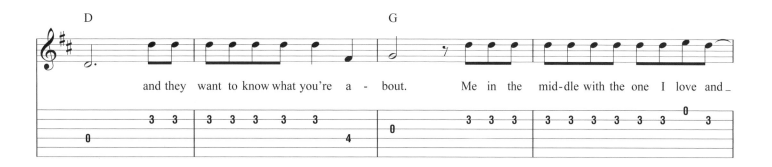

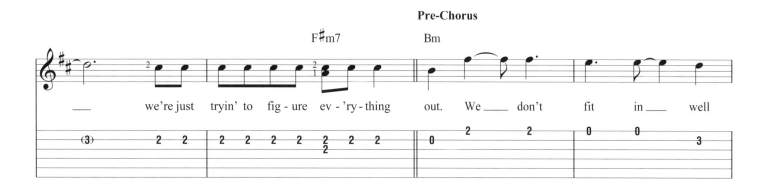

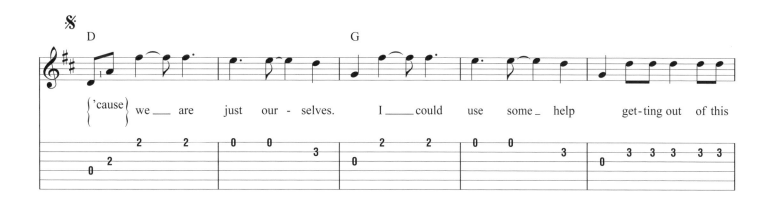

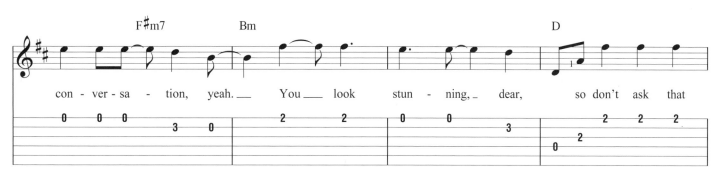

ques - tion _ here. _ This is my on - ly _ fear: that we be - come beau - ti - ful peo -

Chorus

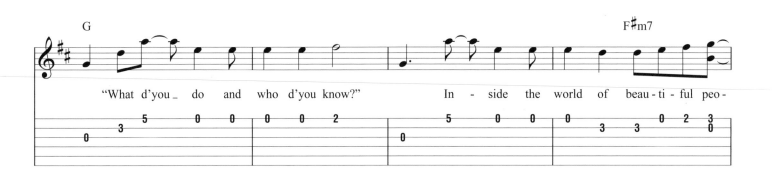

- ple. Drop _ top, de - sign - er clothes, front _ row at fash - ion shows.

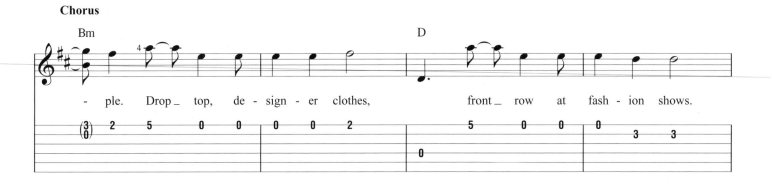

"What d'you _ do and who d'you know?" In - side the world of beau - ti - ful peo -

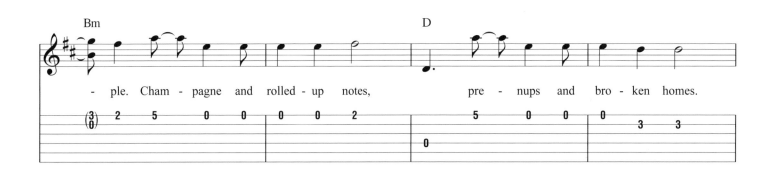

- ple. Cham - pagne and rolled - up notes, pre - nups and bro - ken homes.

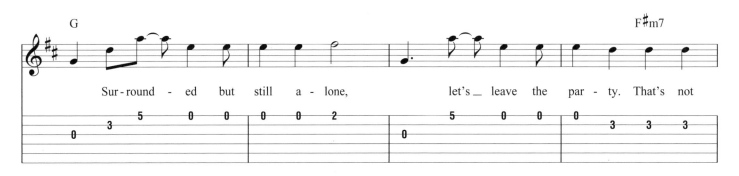

Sur - round - ed but still a - lone, let's _ leave the par - ty. That's not

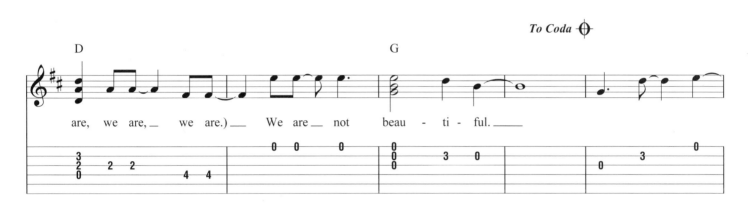

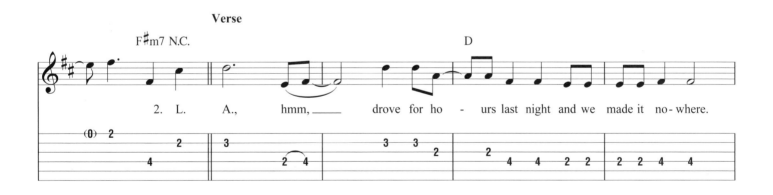

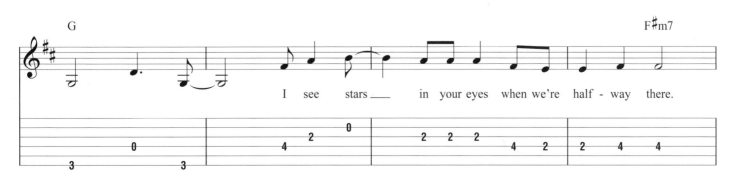

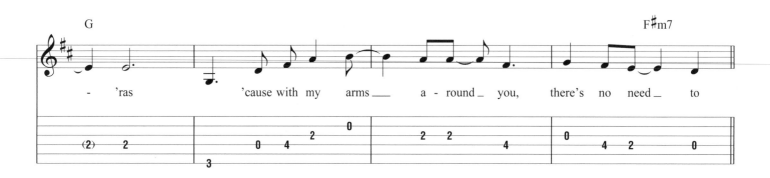

Pre-Chorus

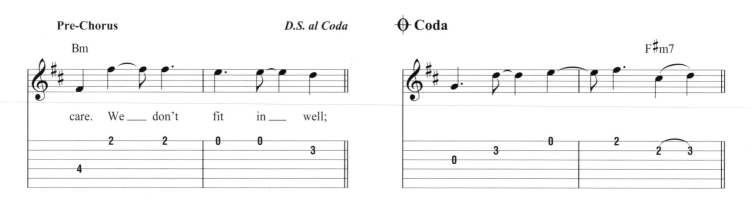

Outro

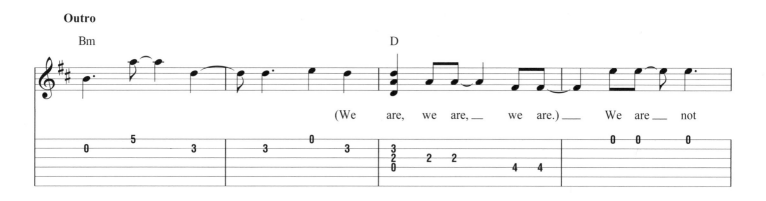

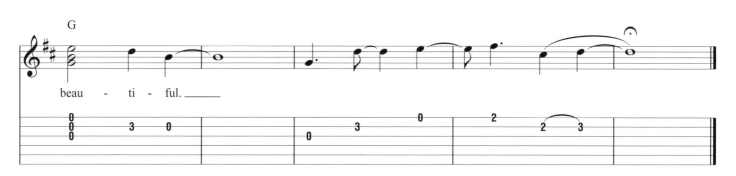

Blinding Lights

Words and Music by Abel Tesfaye, Max Martin, Jason Quenneville, Oscar Holter and Ahmad Balshe

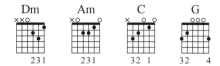

*Capo III

Strum Pattern: 5
Pick Pattern: 1

Intro
Fast

*Optional: To match recording, place capo at 3rd fret.

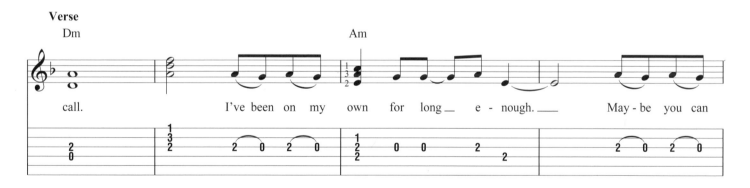

1. I've been try - na

Verse

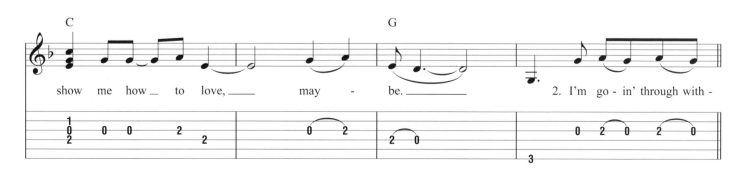

call. I've been on my own for long __ e - nough. __ May - be you can

show me how __ to love, __ may - be. __ 2. I'm go - in' through with -

Verse

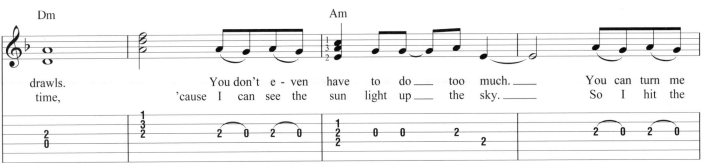

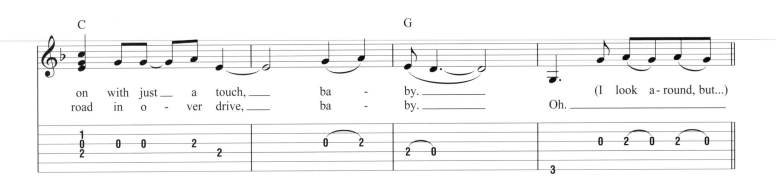

Pre-Chorus

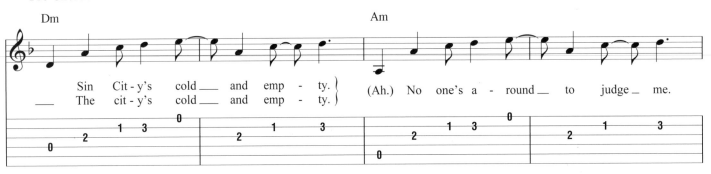

Chorus

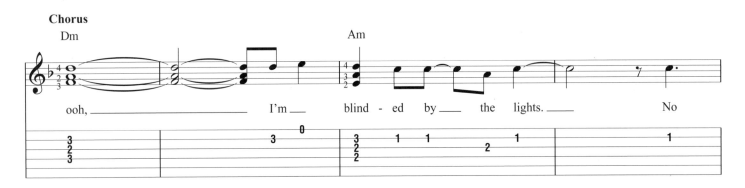

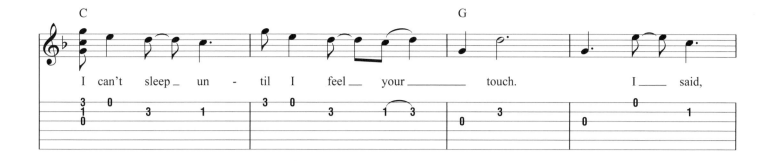

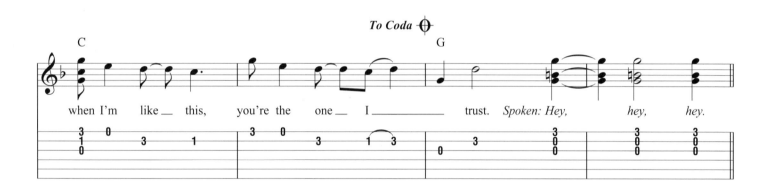

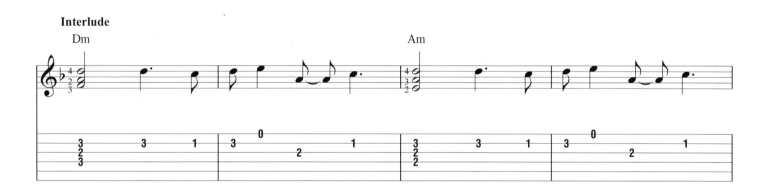

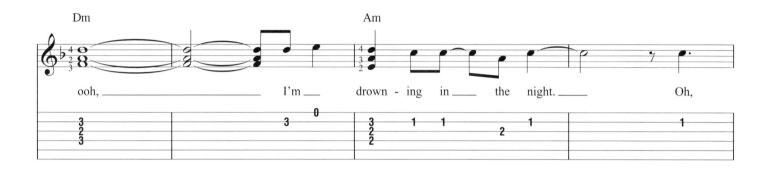

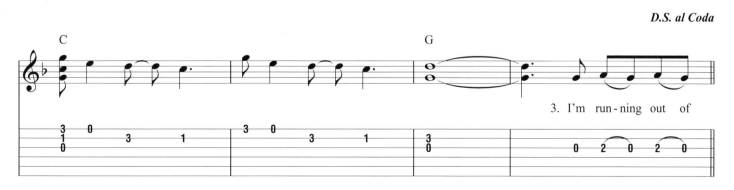

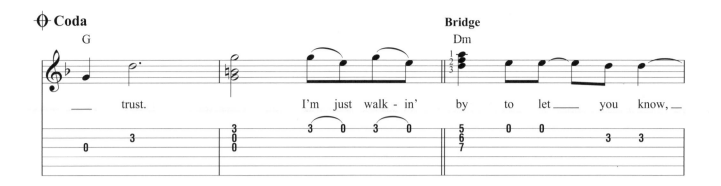

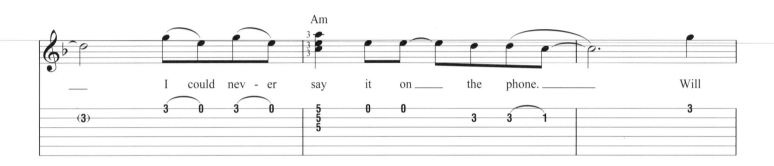

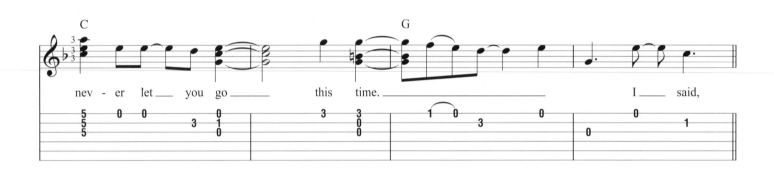

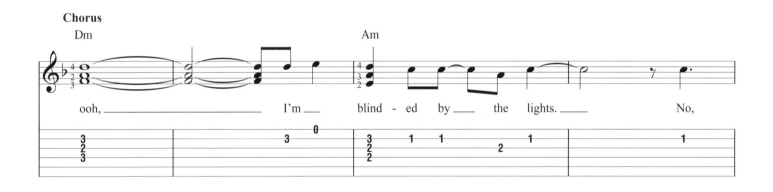

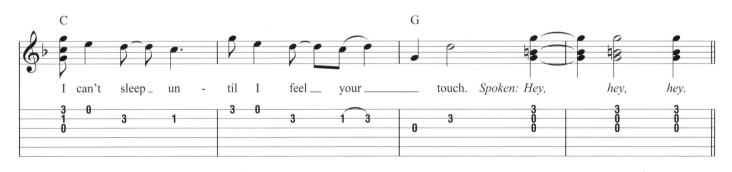

Outro

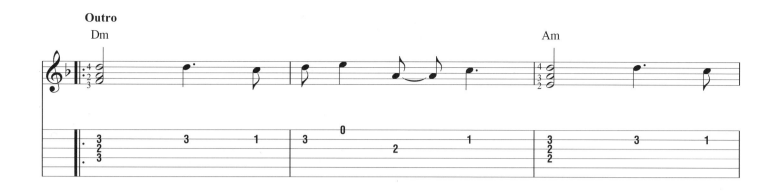

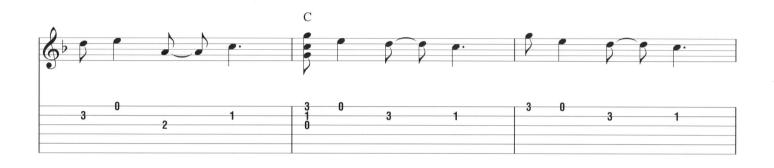

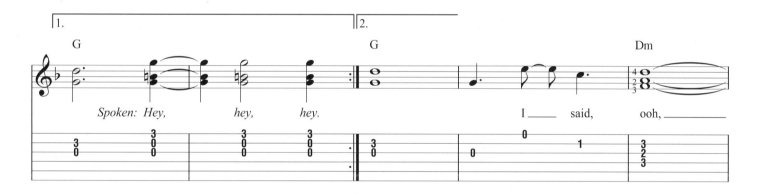

Spoken: Hey, hey, hey. I said, ooh,

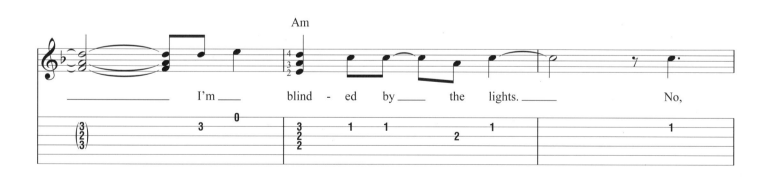

I'm blind - ed by the lights. No,

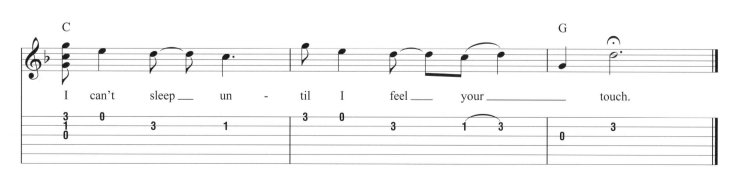

I can't sleep un - til I feel your touch.

Circles

**Words and Music by Austin Post, Kaan Gunesberk,
Louis Bell, William Walsh and Adam Feeney**

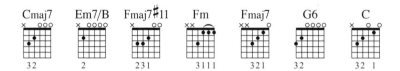

*Tune down 1/2 step:
(low to high) E♭-A♭-D♭-G♭-B♭-E♭

Strum Pattern: 5, 1
Pick Pattern: 1, 4

Intro
Moderately fast

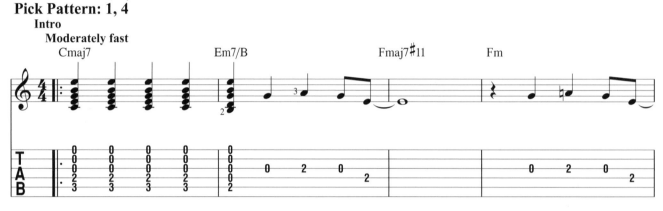

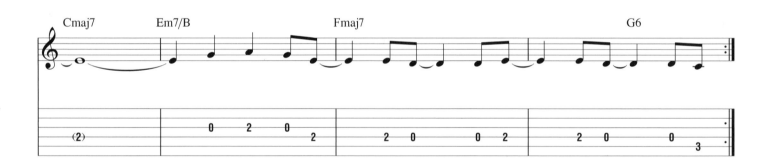

Verse

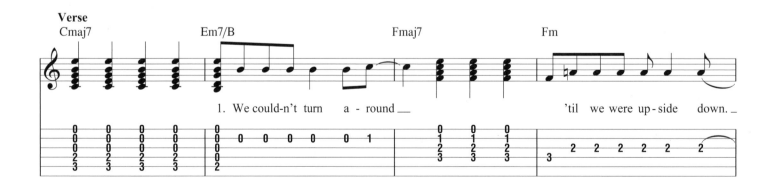

1. We could-n't turn a - round ___ 'til we were up-side down. ___

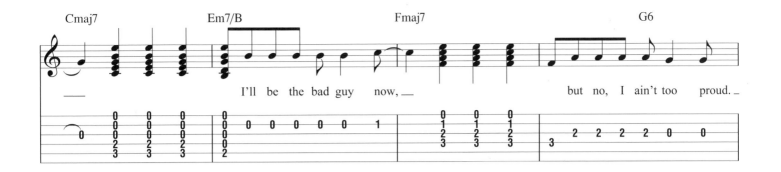

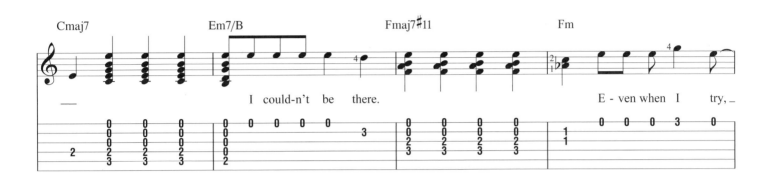

Chorus

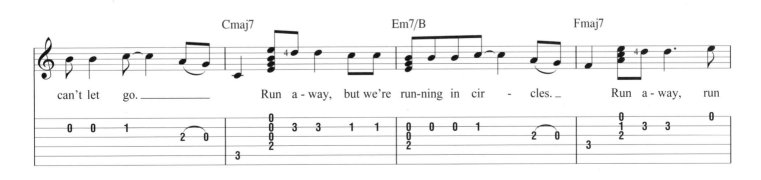

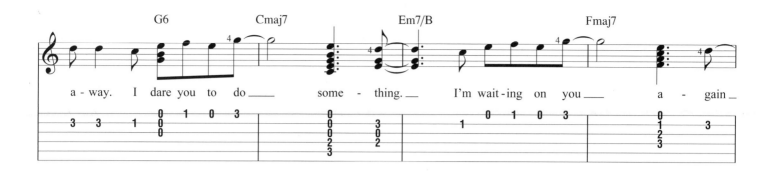

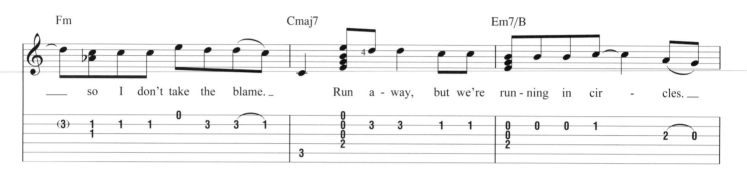

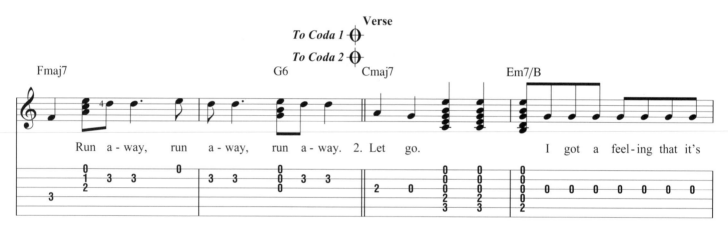

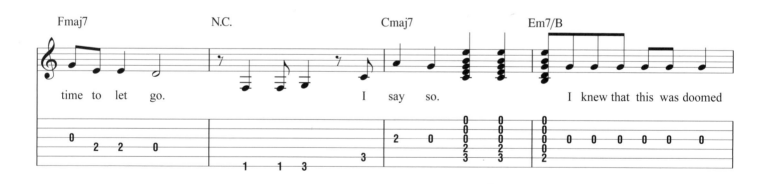

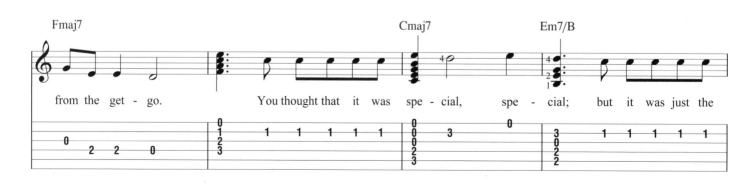

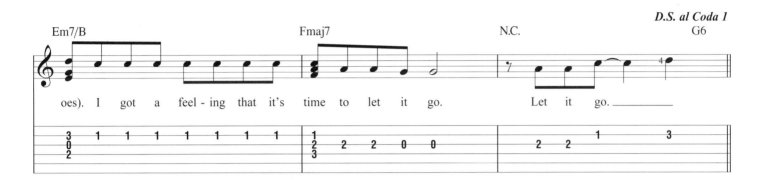

D.S. al Coda 1

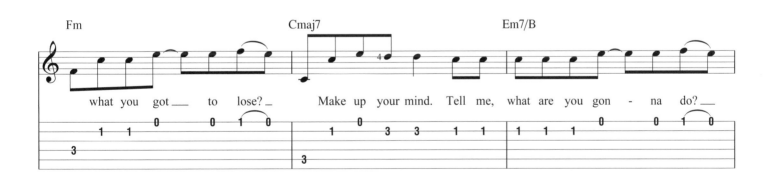

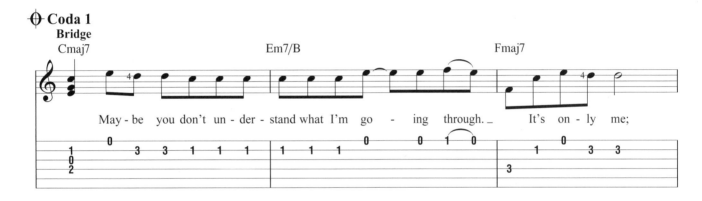

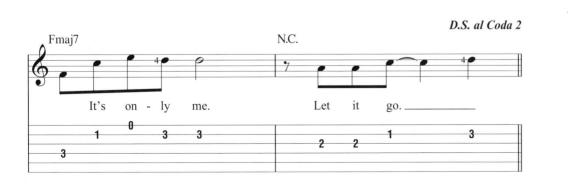

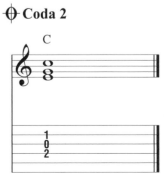

Dance Monkey

Words and Music by Toni Watson

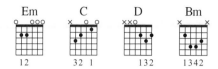

*Capo II

Strum Pattern: 3, 4
Pick Pattern: 3, 4

Intro
Moderately, in 2

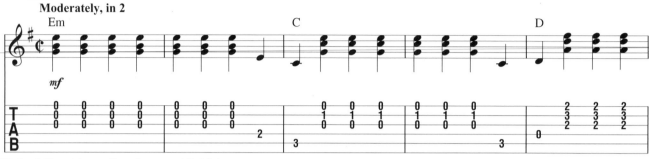

*Optional: To match recording, place capo at 2nd fret.

1. They say, "Oh, my God, I see the way you
2. *See additional lyrics*

**Sung one octave higher.

shine. Take your hands, my dear, and place them both in

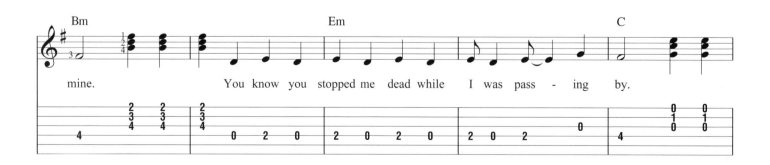

mine. You know you stopped me dead while I was pass - ing by.

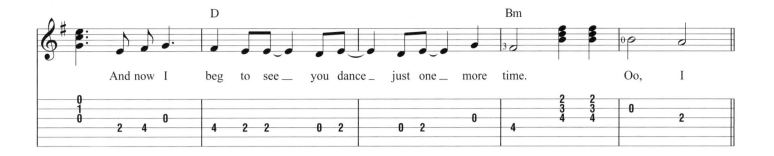

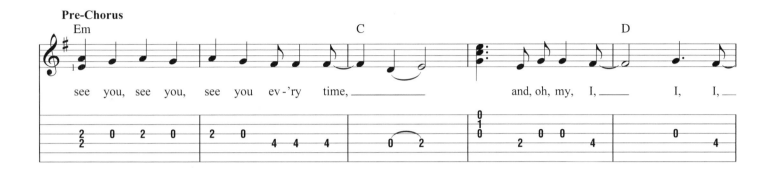

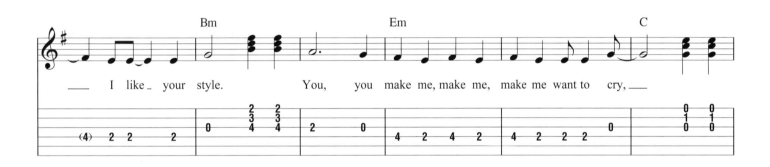

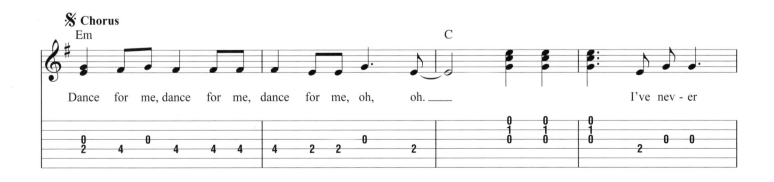

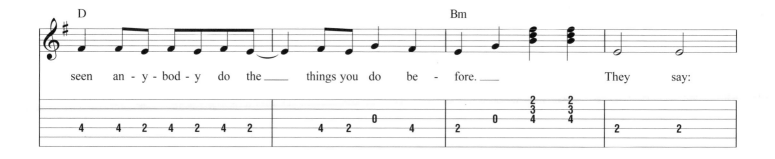

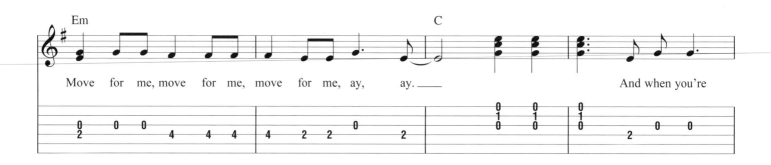

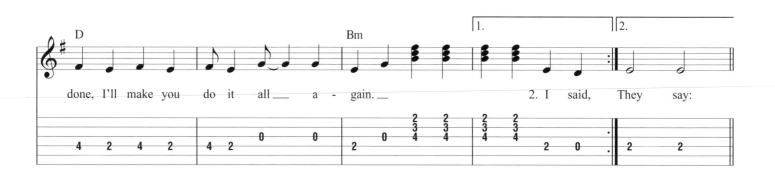

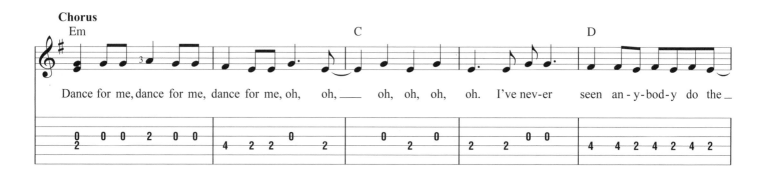

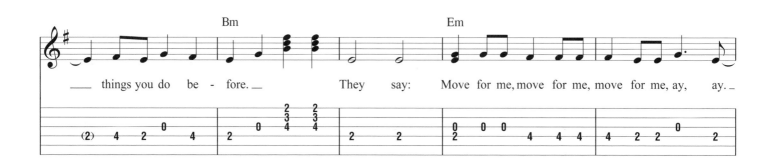

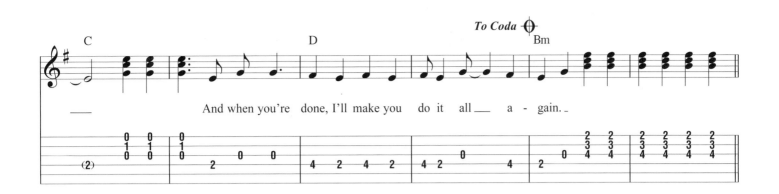

And when you're done, I'll make you do it all ____ a - gain. ____

Bridge

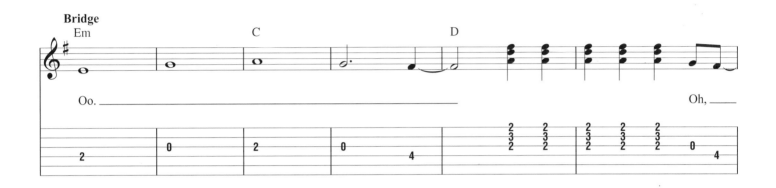

Oo. _____ Oh, ____

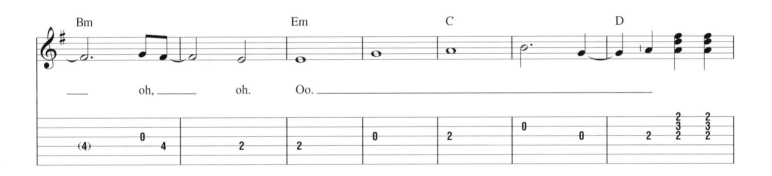

____ oh, _____ oh. Oo. _____

 **Coda**

D.S. al Coda
(take 2nd ending)

Oh, ah, ah. They say:

gain, ____ all ____ a - gain.

Additional Lyrics

2. I said, "Oh, my God, I see you walking by.
Take my hands, my dear, and look me in my eyes."
Just like a monkey, I've been dancing my whole life.
But you just beg to see me dance just one more time.

everything I wanted

Words and Music by Billie Eilish O'Connell and Finneas O'Connell

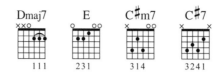

Strum Pattern: 4, 6
Pick Pattern: 1, 6

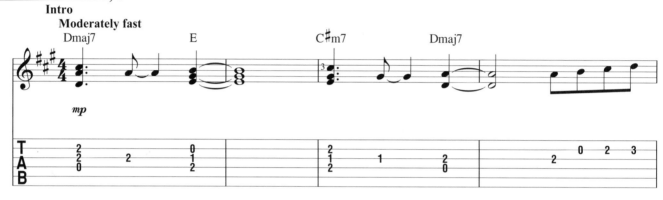

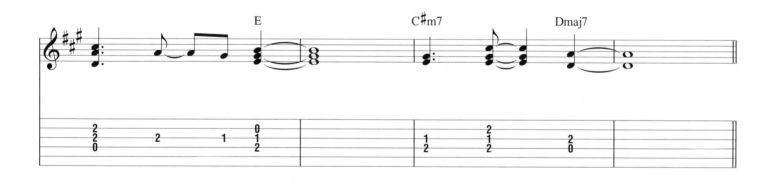

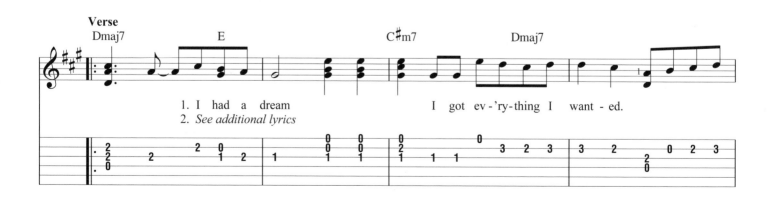

1. I had a dream
2. *See additional lyrics*

I got ev-'ry-thing I want-ed.

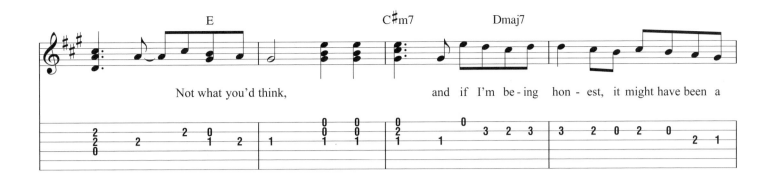

Not what you'd think, and if I'm be-ing hon - est, it might have been a

night - mare to an - y - one who might care.

𝄋 Pre-Chorus

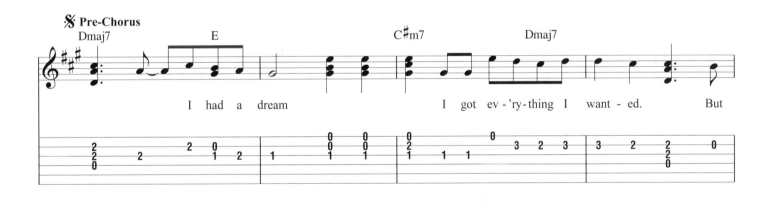

I had a dream I got ev - 'ry-thing I want - ed. But

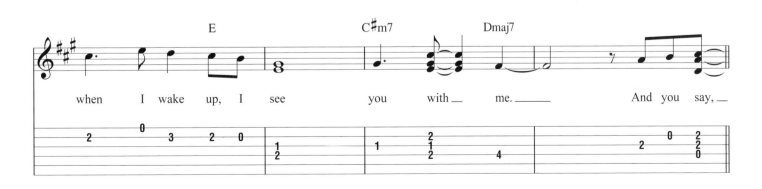

when I wake up, I see you with __ me. _____ And you say, __

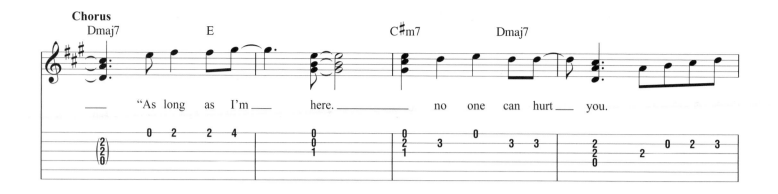

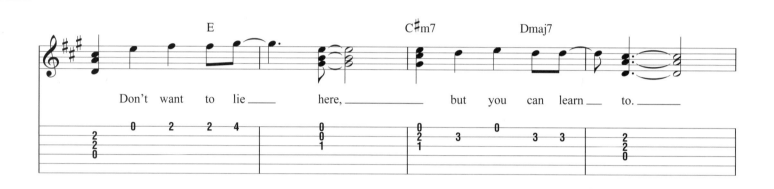

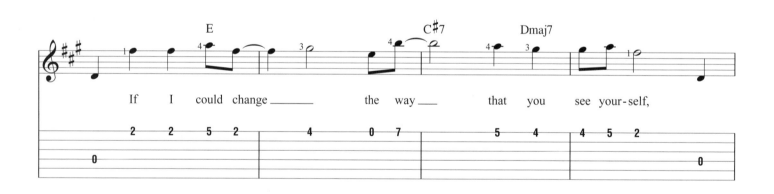

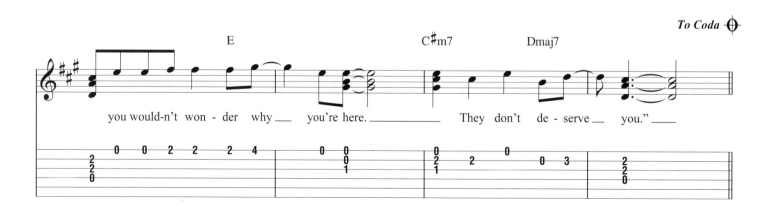

Verse

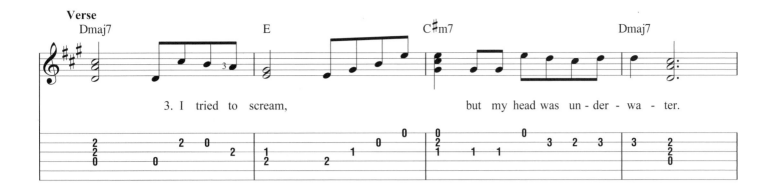

3. I tried to scream, but my head was un-der-wa-ter.

They called me weak like I'm not just some-bod-y's daugh-ter. It could have been a

night-mare, but it felt like they were right there. And it

Bridge

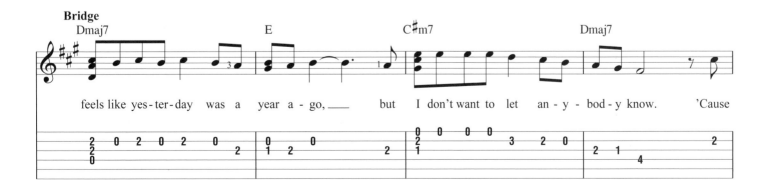

feels like yes-ter-day was a year a-go,___ but I don't want to let an-y-bod-y know. 'Cause

ev -'ry-bod - y wants some-thing from me now, __ and I don't want to let them down. __

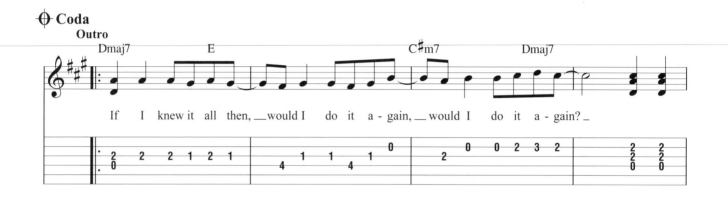

If I knew it all then, __ would I do it a - gain, __ would I do it a - gain? __

If they knew what they said __ would go straight to my head, __ what would they say in - stead? __

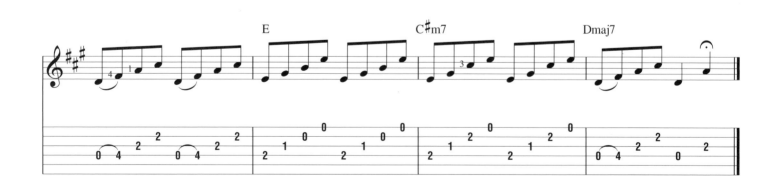

Additional Lyrics

2. Thought I could fly, so I stepped off the Golden, mm.
Nobody cried, nobody even noticed.
I saw them standing right there,
Kinda thought they might care.

Girl

Words and Music by Maren Morris, Sarah Aarons and Greg Kurstin

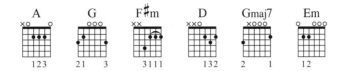

*Capo IV

Strum Pattern: 1, 4
Pick Pattern: 3, 4

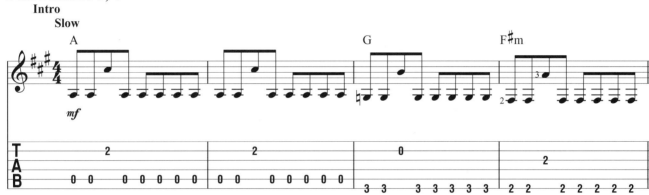

*Optional: To match recording, place capo at 4th fret.

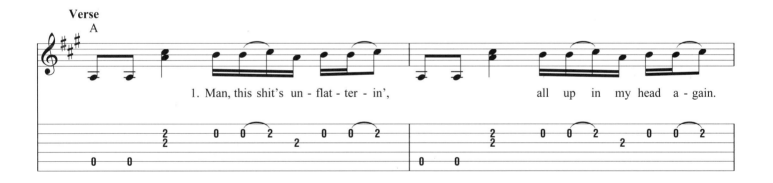

down.　　　If van - i - ty's my vi - ta - min, 　　well, I don't feel the dif - fer - ence.
2. See additional lyrics

I don't like my - self right now. 　　Got - ta find a way out.

What you feel is nat - u - ral, 　　but I don't wan - na feel this an - y - more.

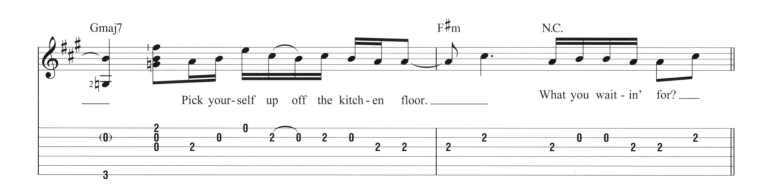

Pick your - self up off the kitch - en floor. 　　What you wait - in' for?

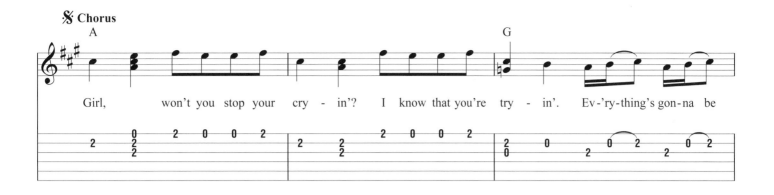

Girl, won't you stop your cry - in'? I know that you're try - in'. Ev-'ry-thing's gon-na be

o - kay,___ ba - by ___ girl. Don't you hang your head low. Don't you lose your

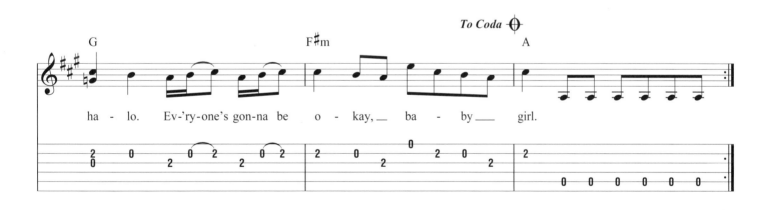

ha - lo. Ev-'ry-one's gon-na be o - kay,___ ba - by ___ girl.

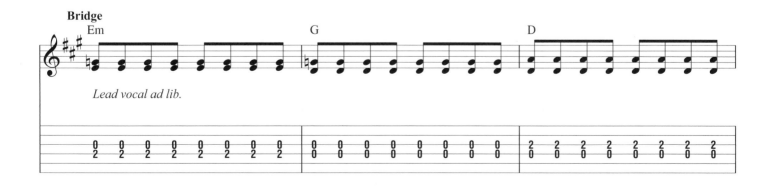

Lead vocal ad lib.

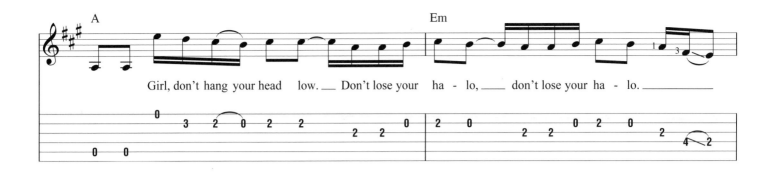

Girl, don't hang your head low. — Don't lose your ha - lo, — don't lose your ha - lo. _____

D.S. al Coda

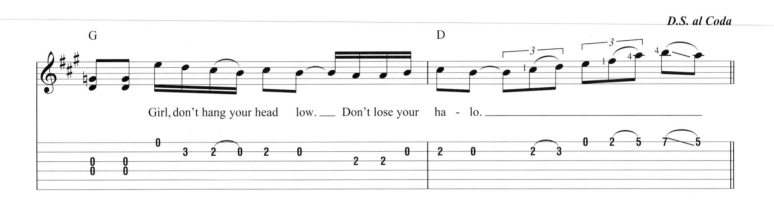

Girl, don't hang your head low. — Don't lose your ha - lo. _____

⊕ Coda
Chorus

girl.   Won't you stop your cry - in'?   I know that you're try - in'.   Ev - ry-thing's gon-na be

o - kay, — ba - by — girl.   Don't you hang your head   low.   Don't you lose your

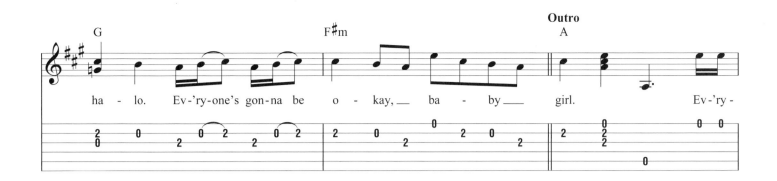

ha - lo. Ev-'ry-one's gon-na be o - kay, __ ba - by __ girl. Ev-'ry-

one's gon - na be _____ o - kay, __ ba - by.

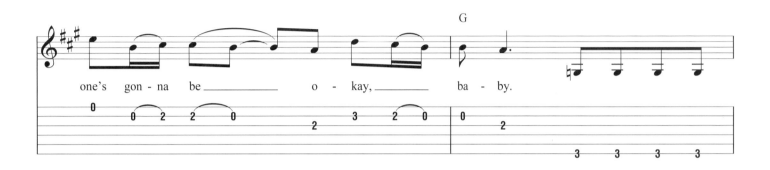

Mm, mm, mm, mm, mm, mm. _____

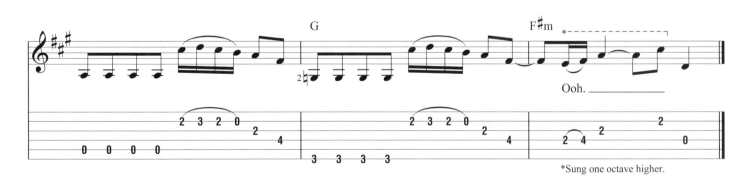

Ooh. _____

*Sung one octave higher.

Additional Lyrics

2. Drawin' your comparisons, tryin' to find who's lesser than.
I don't wanna wear your crown. There's enough to go around.
What you feel is natural. You don't gotta put up with this anymore.
Pick yourself up off the kitchen floor. Tell me what you waitin' for.

Into the Unknown

from FROZEN II
Music and Lyrics by Kristen Anderson-Lopez and Robert Lopez

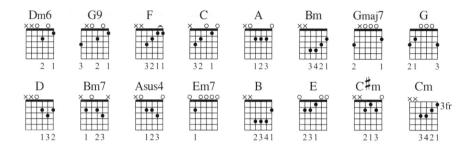

*Capo 1

Strum Pattern: 8
Pick Pattern: 8

Intro
Moderately, in 4

*Optional: To match recording, place capo at 1st fret.

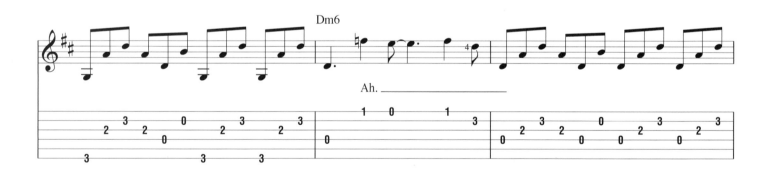

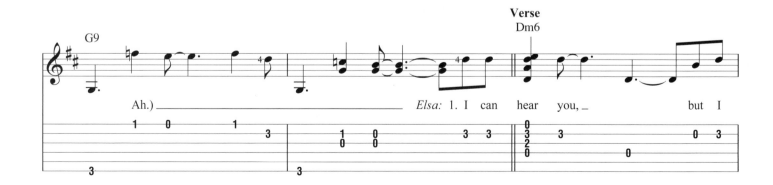

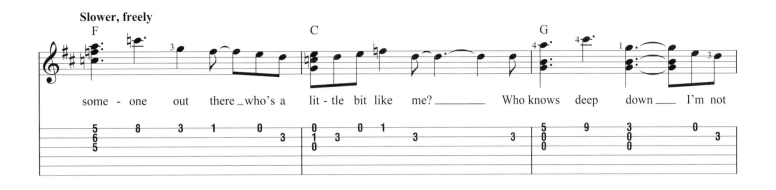

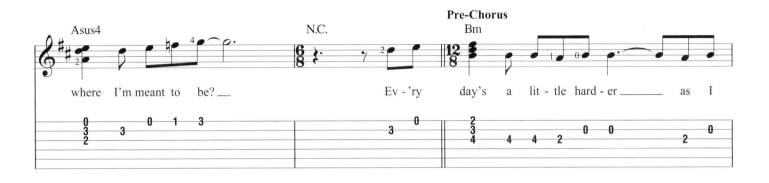

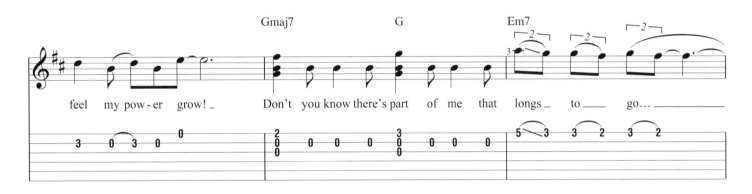

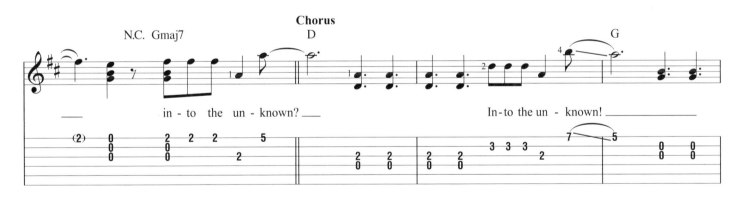

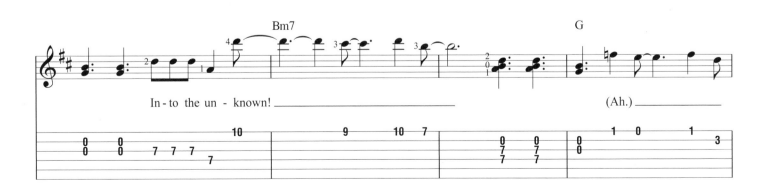

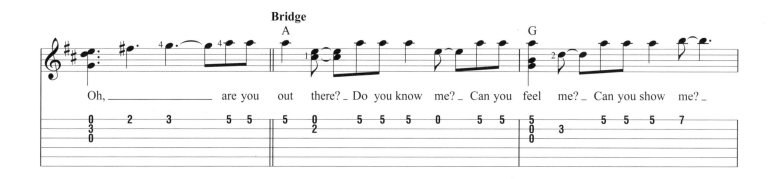

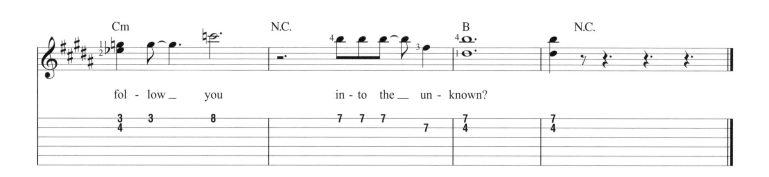

Memories

Words and Music by Adam Levine, Jonathan Bellion, Jordan Johnson, Jacob Hindlin, Stefan Johnson, Michael Pollack and Vincent Ford

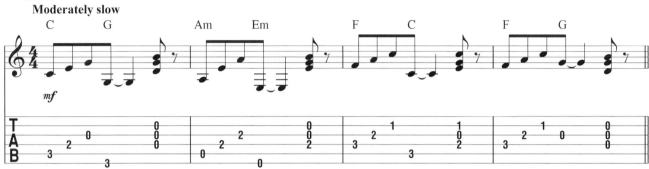

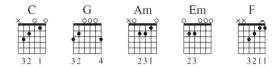

*Tune down 1/2 step:
(low to high) E♭-A♭-D♭-G♭-B♭-E♭

Strum Pattern: 6
Pick Pattern: 5

Intro
Moderately slow

*Optional: To match recording, tune down 1/2 step.

Chorus

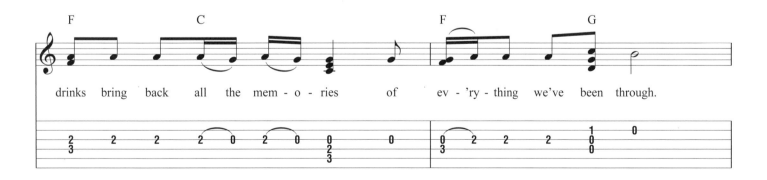

Here's to the ones that we got, cheers to the wish you were here, but you're not. 'Cause the

drinks bring back all the mem-o-ries of ev-'ry-thing we've been through.

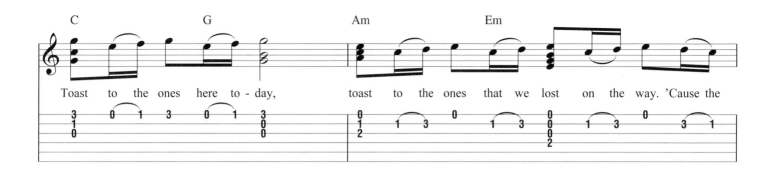

Toast to the ones here to-day, toast to the ones that we lost on the way. 'Cause the

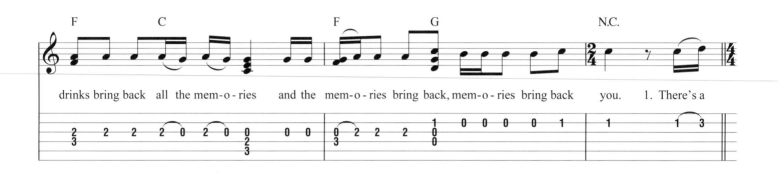

drinks bring back all the mem-o-ries and the mem-o-ries bring back, mem-o-ries bring back you. 1. There's a

Verse

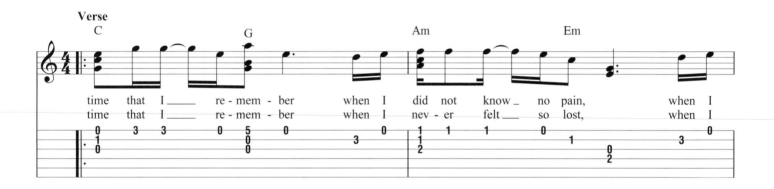

time that I ___ re-mem-ber when I did not know ___ no pain, when I
time that I ___ re-mem-ber when I nev-er felt ___ so lost, when I

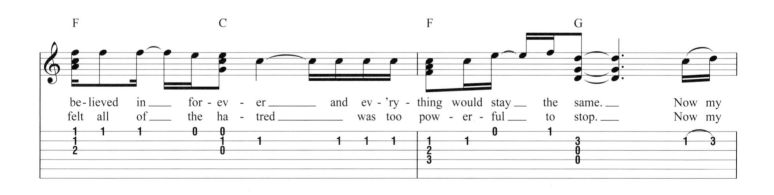

be-lieved in ___ for-ev-er ___ and ev-'ry-thing would stay ___ the same. ___ Now my
felt all of ___ the ha-tred ___ was too pow-er-ful ___ to stop. ___ Now my

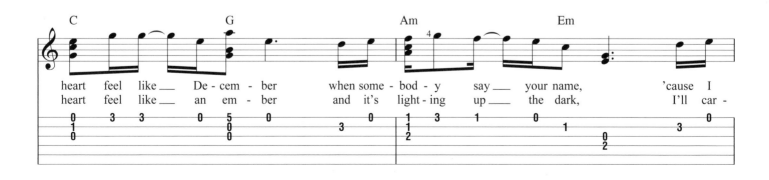

heart feel like ___ De-cem-ber when some-bod-y say ___ your name, 'cause I
heart feel like ___ an em-ber and it's light-ing up ___ the dark, I'll car-

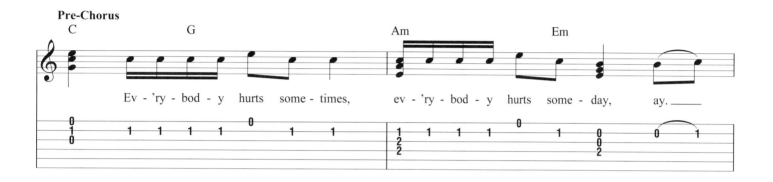

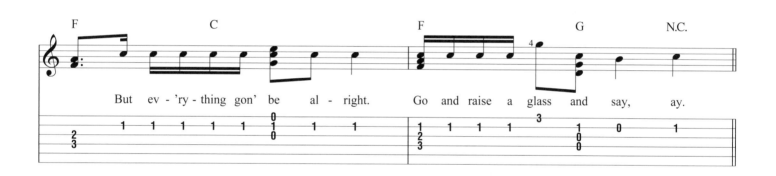

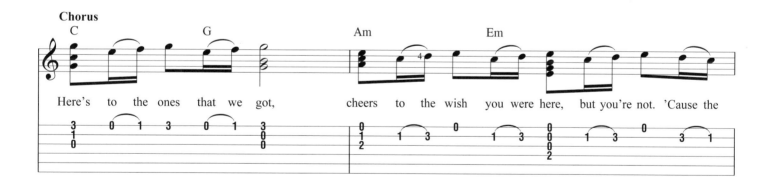

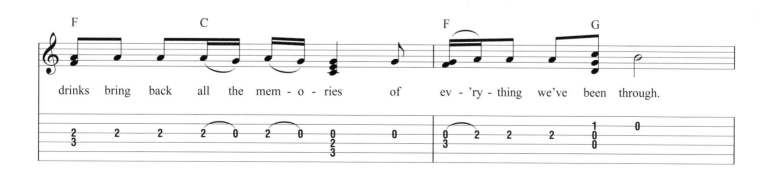

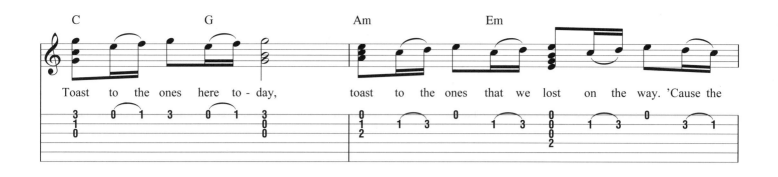

Toast to the ones here to-day, toast to the ones that we lost on the way. 'Cause the

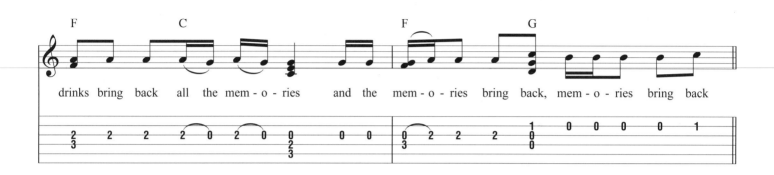

drinks bring back all the mem - o - ries and the mem - o - ries bring back, mem - o - ries bring back

Interlude

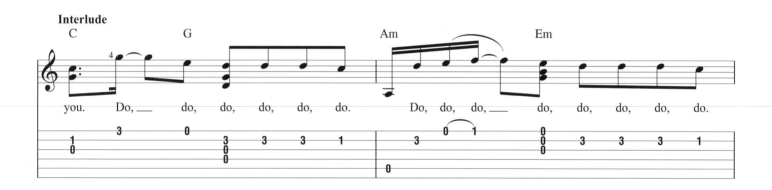

you. Do, __ do, do, do, do, do. Do, do, do, __ do, do, do, do, do.

Do, do, do, __ do, do, do, do. Mem - o - ries bring back, mem - o - ries bring back

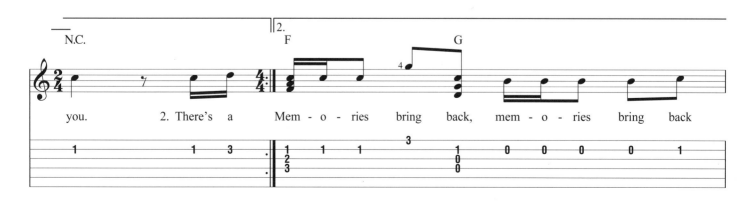

you. 2. There's a Mem - o - ries bring back, mem - o - ries bring back

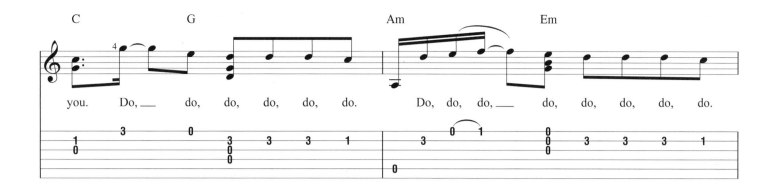

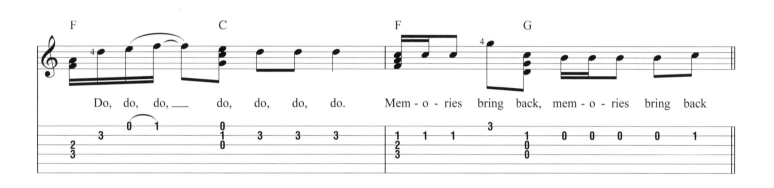

Outro

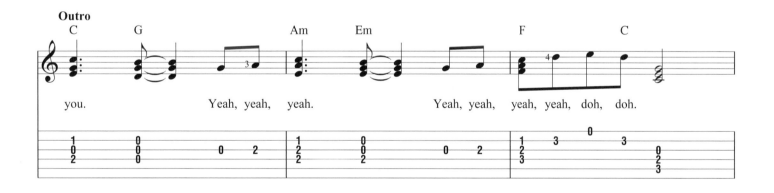

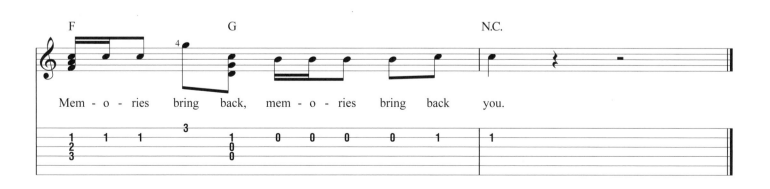

Juice

Words and Music by Lizzo, Theron Makiel Thomas, Eric Frederic, Sam Sumser and Sean Small

*Optional: To match recording, place capo at 1st fret.

Rap 1: *Mir - ror, mir - or on the wall don't say it 'cause I know I'm cute. (Ooh, ba - by.)*
Rap 2: *See additional lyrics*

Lou - is down to my drawers, L. V. all on my shoes. (Ooh, ba - by.)

I be drip - pin' so much sauce go - ta been look - in' like Ra - gu. (Ooh, ba - by.)

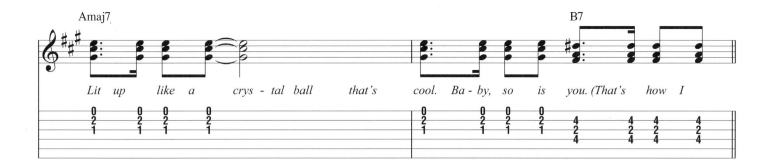

Lit up like a crys - tal ball that's cool. Ba - by, so is you. (That's how I

Pre-Chorus

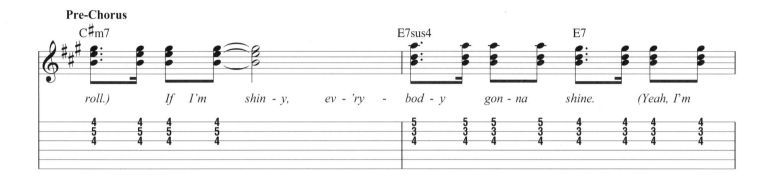

roll.) If I'm shin - y, ev - 'ry - bod - y gon - na shine. (Yeah, I'm

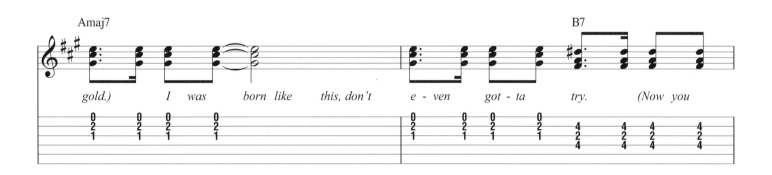

gold.) I was born like this, don't e - ven got - ta try. (Now you

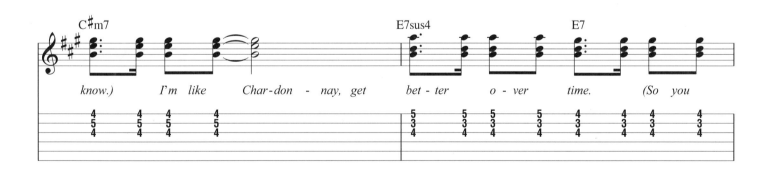

know.) I'm like Char - don - nay, get bet - ter o - ver time. (So you

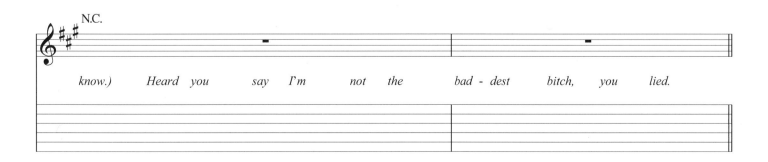

know.) Heard you say I'm not the bad - dest bitch, you lied.

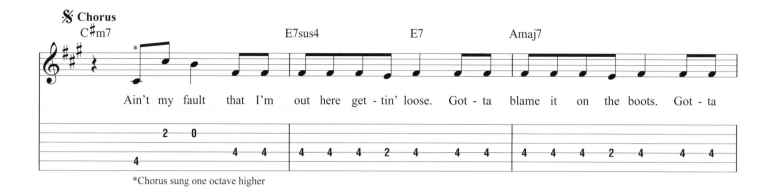

*Chorus sung one octave higher

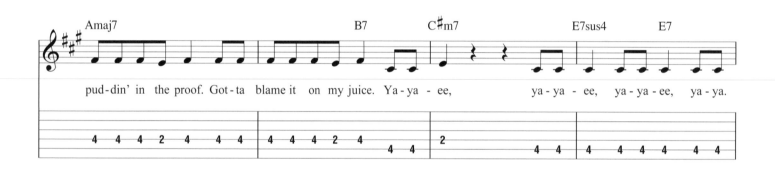

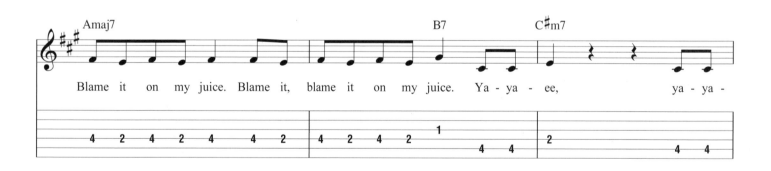

Bridge

N.C.

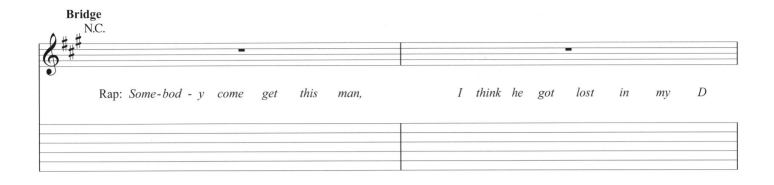

Rap: *Some-bod - y come get this man,* *I think he got lost in my D*

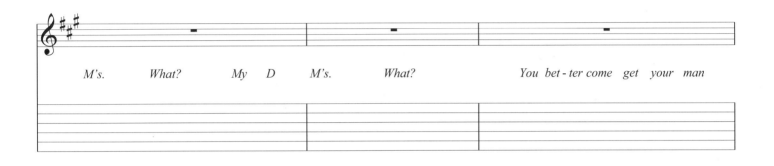

M's. *What?* *My D M's.* *What?* *You bet - ter come get your man*

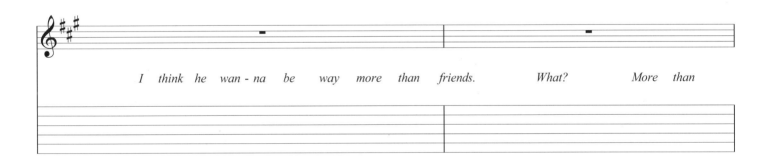

I think he wan - na be way more than friends. *What?* *More than*

$\oplus$ **Coda**

D.S. al Coda

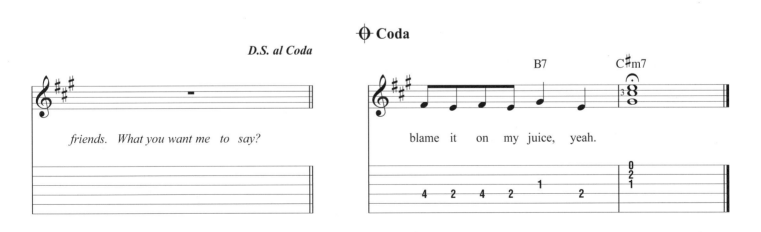

friends. What you want me to say?

B7   C#m7

blame it on my juice, yeah.

Additional Lyrics

Rap 2: *No, I'm not a snack at all. Look, baby, I'm the whole damn meal. (Ooh, baby.)*
Baby, you ain't bein' slick. Don't dare to try to cop a feel. (Ooh, baby.)
The juice ain't worth the squeeze if the juice don't look like this, (like this, like) this, like.
Shut up, nigga, please. Don't make me have to take your bitch.

Lose You to Love Me

Words and Music by Selena Gomez, Justin Tranter, Julia Michaels, Robin Fredriksson and Mattias Larsson

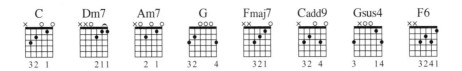

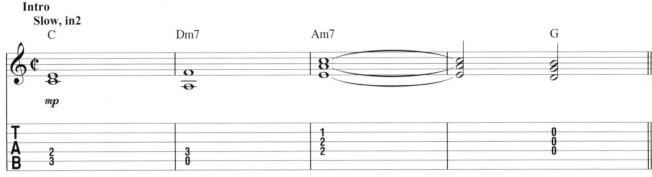

*Capo IV

Strum Pattern: 3
Pick Pattern: 3

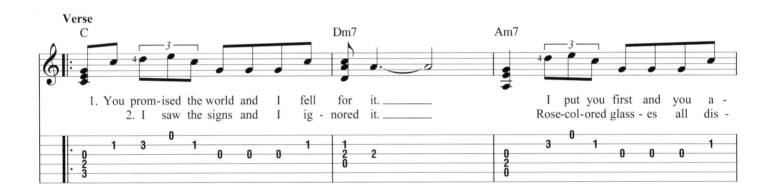

*Optional: To match recording, place capo at 4th fret.

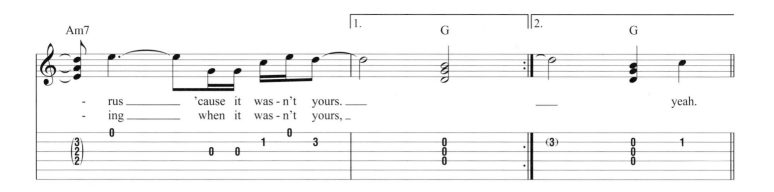

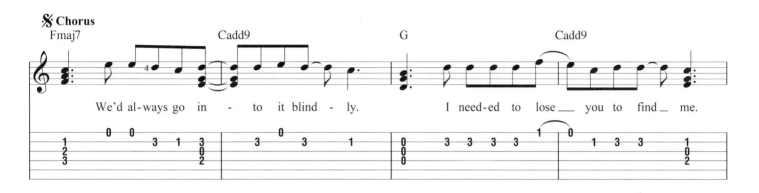

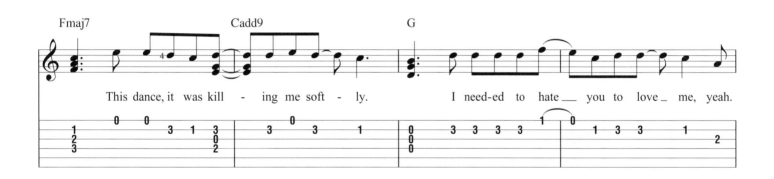

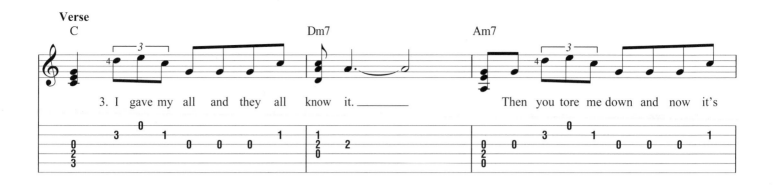

3. I gave my all and they all know it. _____ Then you tore me down and now it's

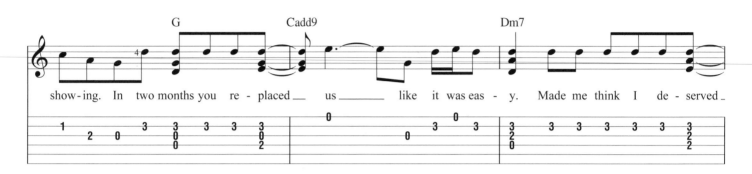

show-ing. In two months you re-placed___ us _____ like it was eas - y. Made me think I de-served _

D.S. al Coda

⊕ **Coda**

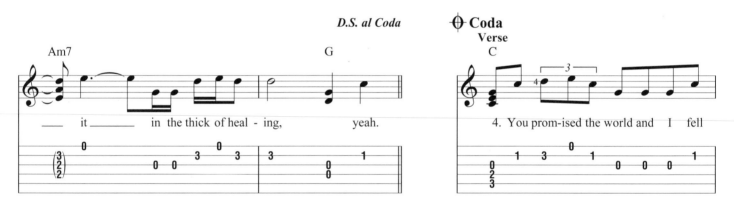

___ it _____ in the thick of heal - ing, yeah.

4. You prom-ised the world and I fell

for it. _____ I put you first and you a - dored it. Set fires to my for -

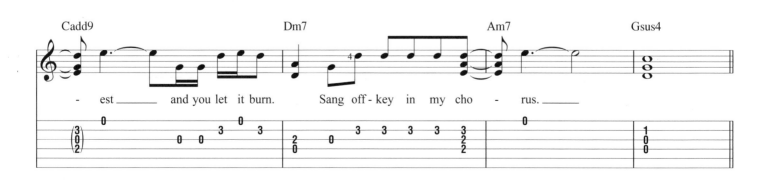

- est _____ and you let it burn. Sang off - key in my cho - rus. _____

Outro

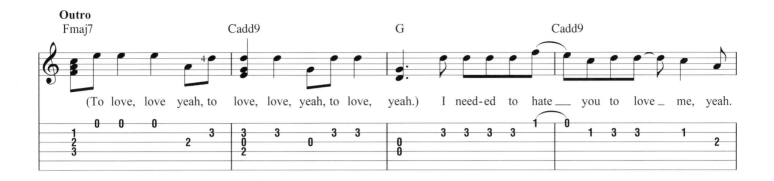

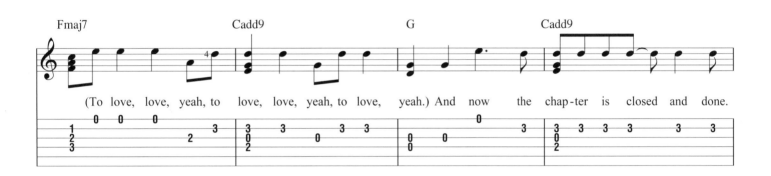

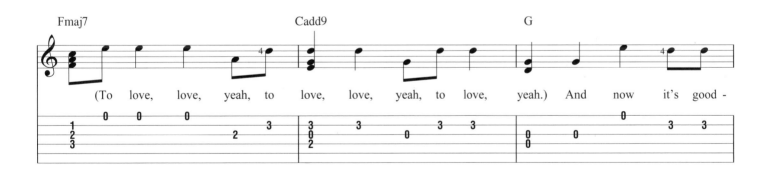

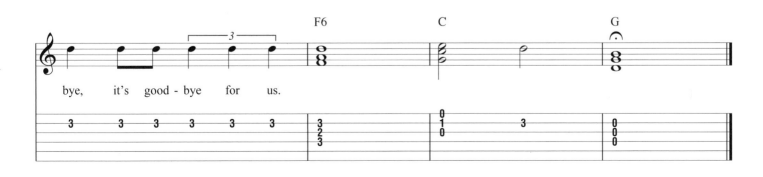

Lover

Words and Music by Taylor Swift

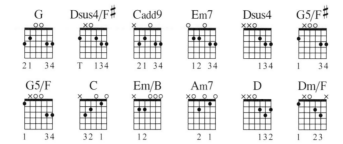

Strum Pattern: 7,
Pick Pattern: 7, 8

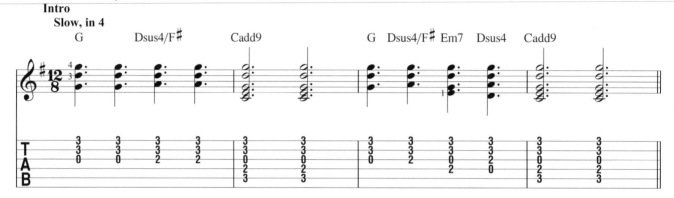

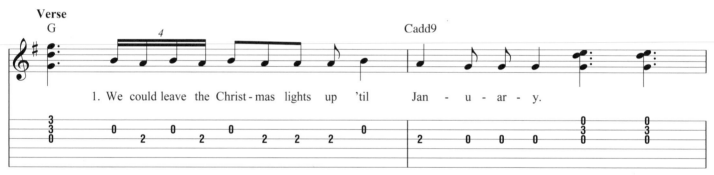

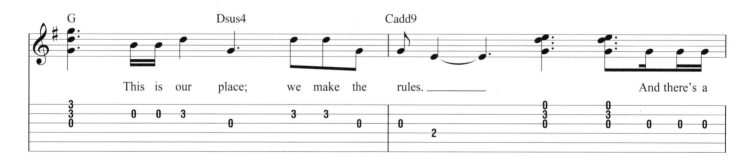

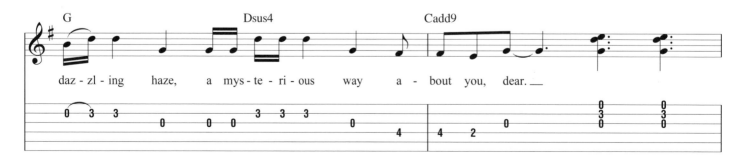

*Vocal octaves in Bridge arr. for playability.

Swear to be o - ver - dra - mat - ic and true ___ to my lov - er. ___ And

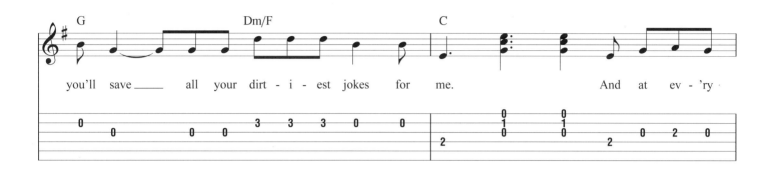

you'll save ___ all your dirt - i - est jokes for me. And at ev - 'ry

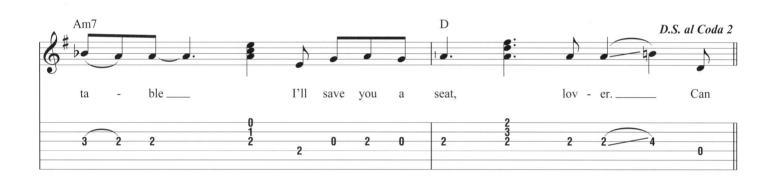

D.S. al Coda 2

ta - ble ___ I'll save you a seat, lov - er. ___ Can

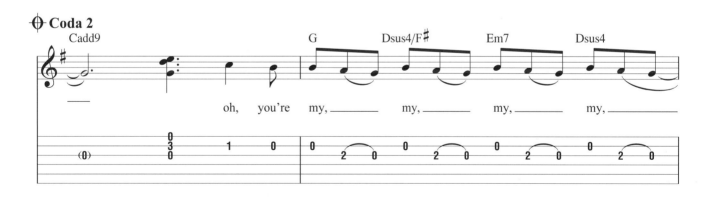

⊕ Coda 2

oh, you're my, ___ my, ___ my, ___ my, ___

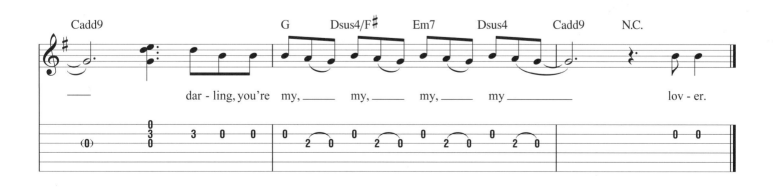

___ dar - ling, you're my, ___ my, ___ my, ___ my ___ lov - er.

Only Human

Words and Music by Nick Jonas, Joseph Jonas, Shellback and Kevin Jonas

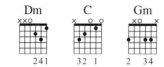

Strum Pattern: 3
Pick Pattern: 2

Intro
Moderately slow

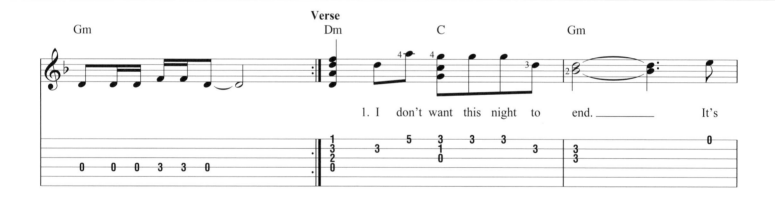

1. I don't want this night to end. _____ It's

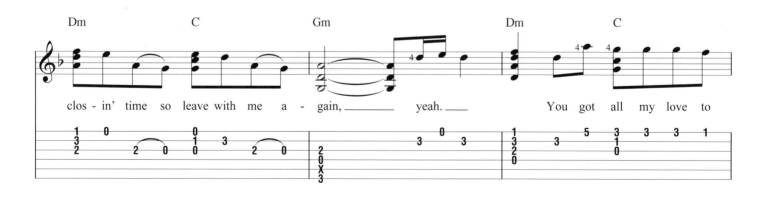

clos-in' time so leave with me a-gain, _____ yeah. _____ You got all my love to

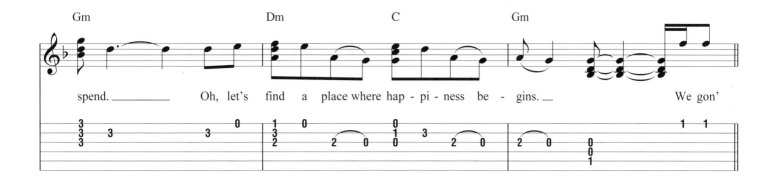

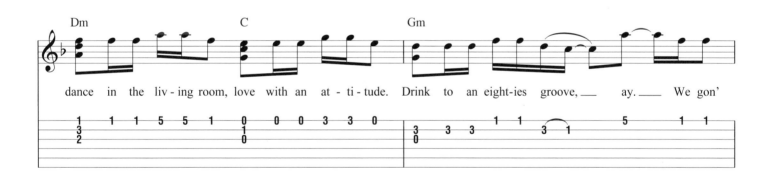

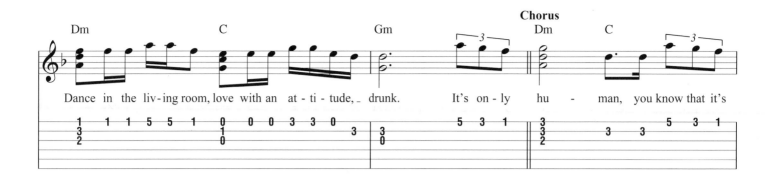

Dance in the liv-ing room, love with an at - ti - tude, _ drunk. It's on - ly hu - man, you know that it's

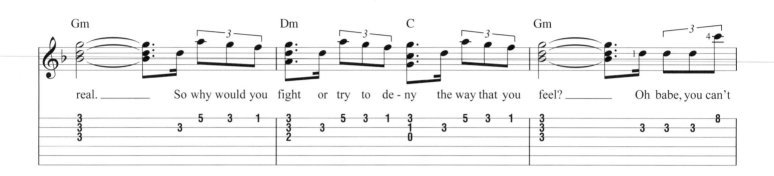

real. _____ So why would you fight or try to de - ny the way that you feel? _____ Oh babe, you can't

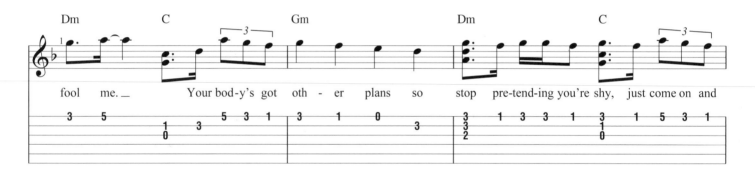

fool me. _ Your bod-y's got oth - er plans so stop pre-tend-ing you're shy, just come on and

To Coda ⊕
Interlude

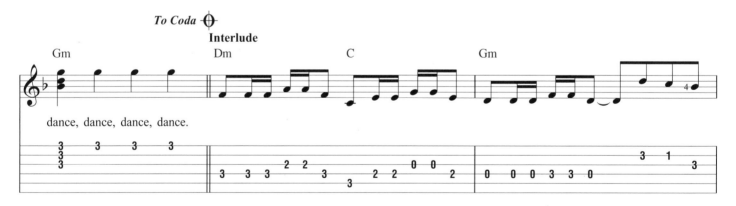

dance, dance, dance, dance.

Verse

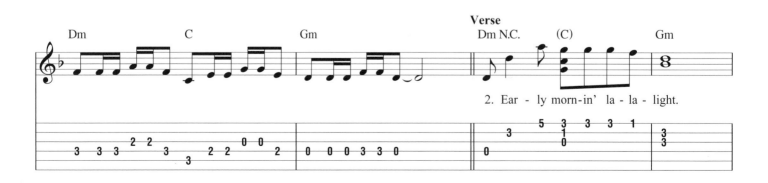

2. Ear - ly morn-in' la - la - light.

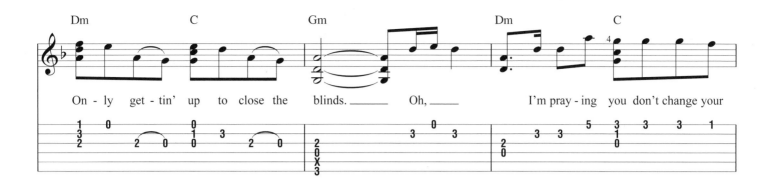

On - ly get - tin' up to close the blinds._____ Oh,_____ I'm pray - ing you don't change your

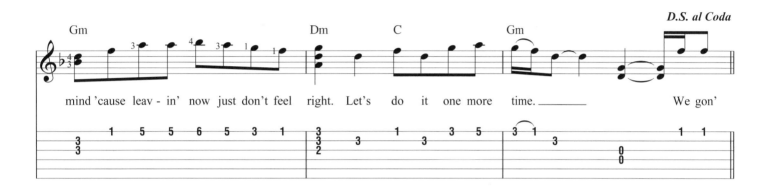

D.S. al Coda

mind 'cause leav - in' now just don't feel right. Let's do it one more time._____ We gon'

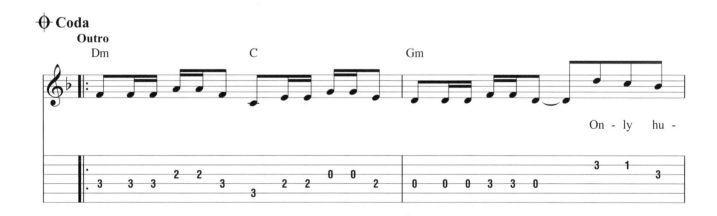

Coda

Outro

On - ly hu -

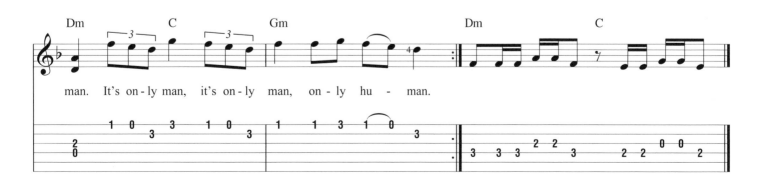

man. It's on - ly man, it's on - ly man, on - ly hu - man.

10,000 Hours

**Words and Music by Dan Smyers, Jordan Reynolds,
Shay Mooney, Justin Bieber, Jason Boyd and Jessie Jo Dillon**

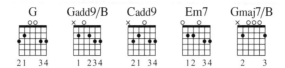

*Capo III

Strum Pattern: 6
Pick Pattern: 4

Verse

Moderately slow

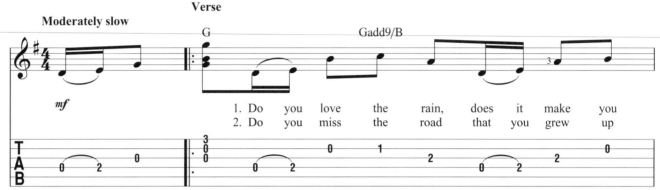

1. Do you love the rain, does it make you
2. Do you miss the road that you grew up

*Optional: To match recording, place capo at 3rd fret.

dance when you're drunk with your friends at a par-ty? What's your fa-v'rite song, does it make you
on? Did you get your mid-dle name from your grand-ma? When you think a-bout your for-ev-er

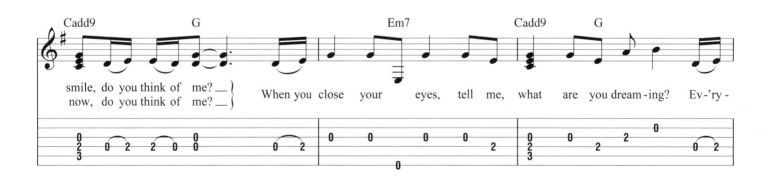

smile, do you think of me? __ } When you close your eyes, tell me, what are you dream-ing? Ev-'ry-
now, do you think of me? __ }

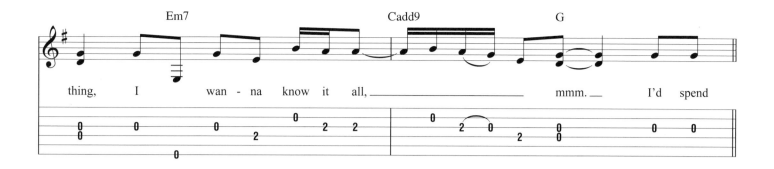

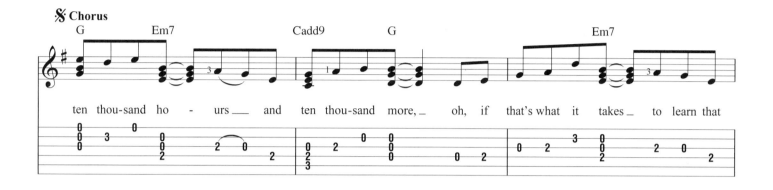

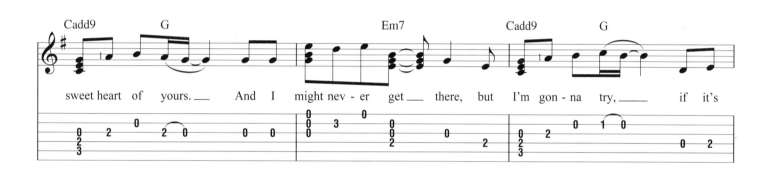

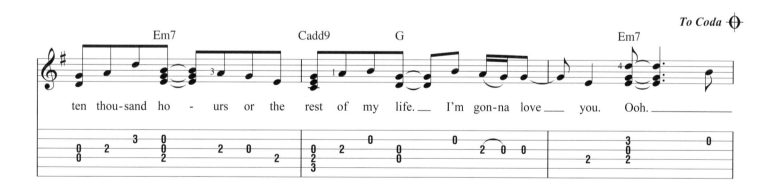

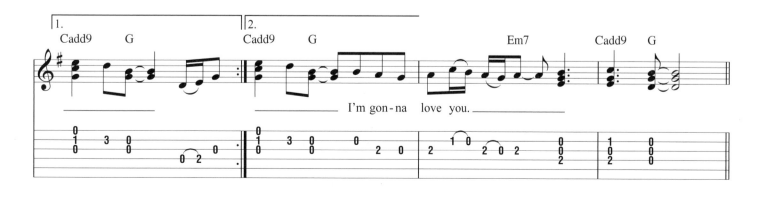

Bridge

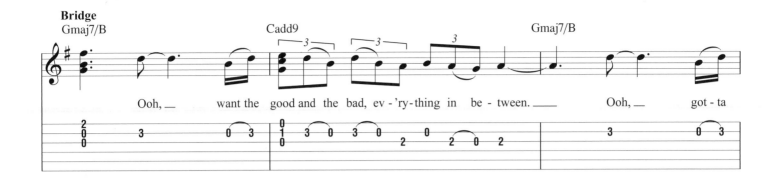

Ooh, ___ want the good and the bad, ev-'ry-thing in be - tween. ___ Ooh, ___ got - ta

D.S. al Coda

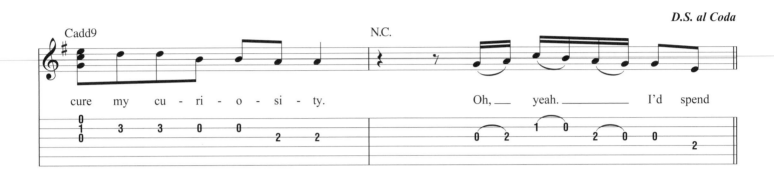

cure my cu - ri - o - si - ty. Oh, ___ yeah. ___ I'd spend

⊕ Coda

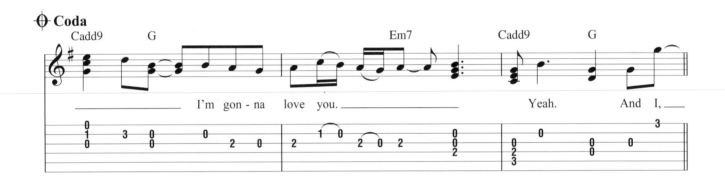

___ I'm gon - na love you. ___ Yeah. And I,

Outro

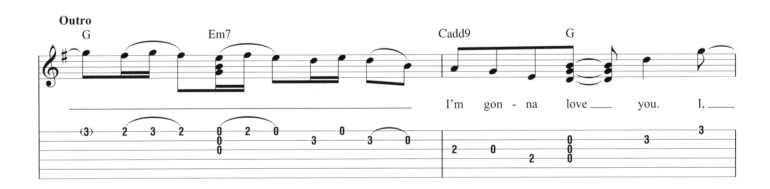

I'm gon - na love ___ you. I, ___

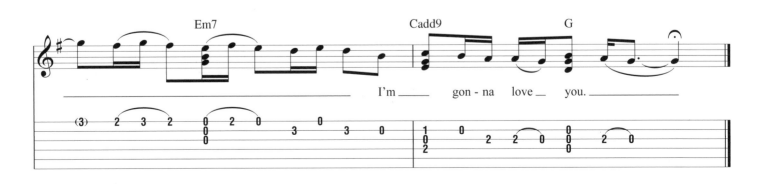

I'm ___ gon - na love ___ you. ___

EASY GUITAR WITH NOTES & TAB

This series features simplified arrangements with notes, tab, chord charts, and strum and pick patterns.

MIXED FOLIOS

00702287	Acoustic	$16.99
00702002	Acoustic Rock Hits for Easy Guitar	$15.99
00702166	All-Time Best Guitar Collection	$19.99
00702232	Best Acoustic Songs for Easy Guitar	$14.99
00119835	Best Children's Songs	$16.99
00702233	Best Hard Rock Songs	$15.99
00703055	The Big Book of Nursery Rhymes & Children's Songs	$16.99
00322179	The Big Easy Book of Classic Rock Guitar	$24.95
00698978	Big Christmas Collection	$17.99
00702394	Bluegrass Songs for Easy Guitar	$12.99
00289632	Bohemian Rhapsody	$17.99
00703387	Celtic Classics	$14.99
00224808	Chart Hits of 2016-2017	$14.99
00267383	Chart Hits of 2017-2018	$14.99
00702149	Children's Christian Songbook	$9.99
00702028	Christmas Classics	$8.99
00101779	Christmas Guitar	$14.99
00702185	Christmas Hits	$10.99
00702141	Classic Rock	$8.95
00159642	Classical Melodies	$12.99
00253933	Disney/Pixar's Coco	$16.99
00702203	CMT's 100 Greatest Country Songs	$29.99

00702283	The Contemporary Christian Collection	$16.99
00196954	Contemporary Disney	$16.99
00702239	Country Classics for Easy Guitar	$22.99
00702257	Easy Acoustic Guitar Songs	$14.99
00702280	Easy Guitar Tab White Pages	$29.99
00702041	Favorite Hymns for Easy Guitar	$10.99
00222701	Folk Pop Songs	$14.99
00140841	4-Chord Hymns for Guitar	$9.99
00702281	4 Chord Rock	$10.99
00126894	Frozen	$14.99
00702286	Glee	$16.99
00699374	Gospel Favorites	$16.99
00702160	The Great American Country Songbook	$16.99
00702050	Great Classical Themes for Easy Guitar	$8.99
00702116	Greatest Hymns for Guitar	$10.99
00275088	The Greatest Showman	$17.99
00148030	Halloween Guitar Songs	$14.99
00702273	Irish Songs	$12.99
00192503	Jazz Classics for Easy Guitar	$14.99
00702275	Jazz Favorites for Easy Guitar	$15.99
00702274	Jazz Standards for Easy Guitar	$16.99
00702162	Jumbo Easy Guitar Songbook	$19.99
00232285	La La Land	$16.99
00702258	Legends of Rock	$14.99
00702189	MTV's 100 Greatest Pop Songs	$24.95

00702272	1950s Rock	$15.99
00702271	1960s Rock	$15.99
00702270	1970s Rock	$16.99
00702269	1980s Rock	$15.99
00702268	1990s Rock	$19.99
00109725	Once	$14.99
00702187	Selections from O Brother Where Art Thou?	$17.99
00702178	100 Songs for Kids	$14.99
00702515	Pirates of the Caribbean	$14.99
00702125	Praise and Worship for Guitar	$10.99
00287930	Songs from *A Star Is Born, The Greatest Showman, La La Land*, and More Movie Musicals	$16.99
00702285	Southern Rock Hits	$12.99
00156420	Star Wars Music	$14.99
00121535	30 Easy Celtic Guitar Solos	$15.99
00702220	Today's Country Hits	$12.99
00121900	Today's Women of Pop & Rock	$14.99
00244654	Top Hits of 2017	$14.99
00283786	Top Hits of 2018	$14.99
00702294	Top Worship Hits	$15.99
00702255	VH1's 100 Greatest Hard Rock Songs	$27.99
00702175	VH1's 100 Greatest Songs of Rock and Roll	$24.99
00702253	Wicked	$12.99

ARTIST COLLECTIONS

00702267	AC/DC for Easy Guitar	$15.99
00702598	Adele for Easy Guitar	$15.99
00156221	Adele – 25	$16.99
00702040	Best of the Allman Brothers	$16.99
00702865	J.S. Bach for Easy Guitar	$14.99
00702169	Best of The Beach Boys	$12.99
00702292	The Beatles — 1	$19.99
00125796	Best of Chuck Berry	$15.99
00702201	The Essential Black Sabbath	$12.95
02501615	Zac Brown Band — The Foundation	$16.99
02501621	Zac Brown Band — You Get What You Give	$16.99
00702043	Best of Johnny Cash	$16.99
00702090	Eric Clapton's Best	$12.99
00702086	Eric Clapton — from the Album Unplugged	$15.99
00702202	The Essential Eric Clapton	$14.99
00702250	blink-182 — Greatest Hits	$15.99
00702053	Best of Patsy Cline	$15.99
00222697	Very Best of Coldplay – 2nd Edition	$14.99
00702229	The Very Best of Creedence Clearwater Revival	$15.99
00702145	Best of Jim Croce	$15.99
00702278	Crosby, Stills & Nash	$12.99
14042809	Bob Dylan	$14.99
00702276	Fleetwood Mac — Easy Guitar Collection	$14.99
00139462	The Very Best of Grateful Dead	$15.99
00702136	Best of Merle Haggard	$14.99
00702227	Jimi Hendrix — Smash Hits	$16.99
00702288	Best of Hillsong United	$12.99
00702236	Best of Antonio Carlos Jobim	$14.99
00702245	Elton John — Greatest Hits 1970–2002	$17.99

00129855	Jack Johnson	$16.99
00702204	Robert Johnson	$10.99
00702234	Selections from Toby Keith — 35 Biggest Hits	$12.95
00702003	Kiss	$12.99
00702216	Lynyrd Skynyrd	$15.99
00702182	The Essential Bob Marley	$14.99
00146081	Maroon 5	$14.99
00121925	Bruno Mars – Unorthodox Jukebox	$12.99
00702248	Paul McCartney — All the Best	$14.99
00702129	Songs of Sarah McLachlan	$12.95
00125484	The Best of MercyMe	$12.99
02501316	Metallica — Death Magnetic	$19.99
00702209	Steve Miller Band — Young Hearts (Greatest Hits)	$12.95
00124167	Jason Mraz	$15.99
00702096	Best of Nirvana	$15.99
00702211	The Offspring — Greatest Hits	$12.95
00138026	One Direction	$14.99
00702030	Best of Roy Orbison	$15.99
00702144	Best of Ozzy Osbourne	$14.99
00702279	Tom Petty	$12.99
00102911	Pink Floyd	$16.99
00702139	Elvis Country Favorites	$16.99
00702293	The Very Best of Prince	$15.99
00699415	Best of Queen for Guitar	$15.99
00109279	Best of R.E.M.	$14.99
00702208	Red Hot Chili Peppers — Greatest Hits	$15.99
00198960	The Rolling Stones	$16.99
00174793	The Very Best of Santana	$14.99
00702196	Best of Bob Seger	$12.95
00146046	Ed Sheeran	$14.99
00702252	Frank Sinatra — Nothing But the Best	$12.99

00702010	Best of Rod Stewart	$16.99
00702049	Best of George Strait	$14.99
00702259	Taylor Swift for Easy Guitar	$15.99
00254499	Taylor Swift – Easy Guitar Anthology	$19.99
00702260	Taylor Swift — Fearless	$14.99
00139727	Taylor Swift — 1989	$17.99
00115960	Taylor Swift — Red	$16.99
00253667	Taylor Swift — Reputation	$17.99
00702290	Taylor Swift — Speak Now	$16.99
00232849	Chris Tomlin Collection – 2nd Edition	$14.99
00702226	Chris Tomlin — See the Morning	$12.95
00148643	Train	$14.99
00702427	U2 — 18 Singles	$16.99
00702108	Best of Stevie Ray Vaughan	$16.99
00279005	The Who	$14.99
00702123	Best of Hank Williams	$14.99
00194548	Best of John Williams	$14.99
00702111	Stevie Wonder — Guitar Collection	$9.95
00702228	Neil Young — Greatest Hits	$15.99
00119133	Neil Young — Harvest	$14.99

Prices, contents and availability subject to change without notice.

Visit Hal Leonard online at **halleonard.com**

0819
306

easy GUITAR play along

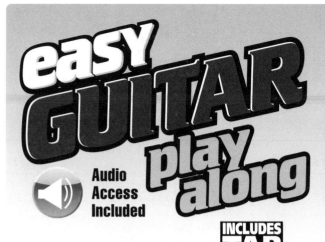

Audio Access Included

INCLUDES TAB

The *Easy Guitar Play Along*® series features streamlined transcriptions of your favorite songs. Just follow the tab, listen to the audio to hear how the guitar should sound, and then play along using the backing tracks. Playback tools are provided for slowing down the tempo without changing pitch and looping challenging parts. The melody and lyrics are included in the book so that you can sing or simply follow along.

1. ROCK CLASSICS
Jailbreak • Living After Midnight • Mississippi Queen • Rocks Off • Runnin' Down a Dream • Smoke on the Water • Strutter • Up Around the Bend.
00702560 Book/CD Pack....... $14.99

2. ACOUSTIC TOP HITS
About a Girl • I'm Yours • The Lazy Song • The Scientist • 21 Guns • Upside Down • What I Got • Wonderwall.
00702569 Book/CD Pack....... $14.99

3. ROCK HITS
All the Small Things • Best of You • Brain Stew (The Godzilla Remix) • Californication • Island in the Sun • Plush • Smells Like Teen Spirit • Use Somebody.
00702570 Book/CD Pack....... $14.99

4. ROCK 'N' ROLL
Blue Suede Shoes • I Get Around • I'm a Believer • Jailhouse Rock • Oh, Pretty Woman • Peggy Sue • Runaway • Wake Up Little Susie.
00702572 Book/CD Pack....... $14.99

6. CHRISTMAS SONGS
Have Yourself a Merry Little Christmas • A Holly Jolly Christmas • The Little Drummer Boy • Run Rudolph Run • Santa Claus Is Comin' to Town • Silver and Gold • Sleigh Ride • Winter Wonderland.
00101879 Book/CD Pack......... $14.99

7. BLUES SONGS FOR BEGINNERS
Come On (Part 1) • Double Trouble • Gangster of Love • I'm Ready • Let Me Love You Baby • Mary Had a Little Lamb • San-Ho-Zay • T-Bone Shuffle.
00103235 Book/Online Audio $14.99

8. ACOUSTIC SONGS FOR BEGINNERS
Barely Breathing • Drive • Everlong • Good Riddance (Time of Your Life) • Hallelujah • Hey There Delilah • Lake of Fire • Photograph.
00103240 Book/CD Pack $15.99

9. ROCK SONGS FOR BEGINNERS
Are You Gonna Be My Girl • Buddy Holly • Everybody Hurts • In Bloom • Otherside • The Rock Show • Santa Monica • When I Come Around.
00103255 Book/CD Pack.....$14.99

10. GREEN DAY
Basket Case • Boulevard of Broken Dreams • Good Riddance (Time of Your Life) • Holiday • Longview • 21 Guns • Wake Me up When September Ends • When I Come Around.
00122322 Book/CD Pack $14.99

11. NIRVANA
All Apologies • Come As You Are • Heart Shaped Box • Lake of Fire • Lithium • The Man Who Sold the World • Rape Me • Smells Like Teen Spirit.
00122325 Book/Online Audio $14.99

13. AC/DC
Back in Black • Dirty Deeds Done Dirt Cheap • For Those About to Rock (We Salute You) • Hells Bells • Highway to Hell • Rock and Roll Ain't Noise Pollution • T.N.T. • You Shook Me All Night Long.
14042895 Book/Online Audio........$16.99

14. JIMI HENDRIX – SMASH HITS
All Along the Watchtower • Can You See Me • Crosstown Traffic • Fire • Foxey Lady • Hey Joe • Manic Depression • Purple Haze • Red House • Remember • Stone Free • The Wind Cries Mary.
00130591 Book/Online Audio........$24.99

HAL•LEONARD®
www.halleonard.com

Prices, contents, and availability subject to change without notice.

FIRST 50

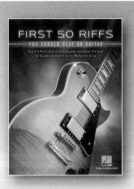

Books in the First 50 series contain easy to intermediate arrangements for must-know songs. Each arrangement is simple and streamlined, yet still captures the essence of the tune.

First 50 Bluegrass Solos You Should Play on Guitar
I Am a Man of Constant Sorrow • Long Journey Home • Molly and Tenbrooks • Old Joe Clark • Rocky Top • Salty Dog Blues • and more!
00298574 Solo Guitar $14.99

First 50 Blues Songs You Should Play on Guitar
All Your Love (I Miss Loving) • Bad to the Bone • Born Under a Bad Sign • Dust My Broom • Hoodoo Man Blues • Little Red Rooster • Love Struck Baby • Pride and Joy • Smoking Gun • Still Got the Blues • The Thrill Is Gone • You Shook Me • and many more.
00235790 Guitar $14.99

First 50 Blues Turnarounds You Should Play on Guitar
You'll learn cool turnarounds in the styles of these jazz legends: John Lee Hooker, Robert Johnson, Joe Pass, Jimmy Rogers, Hubert Sumlin, Stevie Ray Vaughan, T-Bone Walker, Muddy Waters, and more!
00277469 Guitar $14.99

First 50 Chords You Should Play on Guitar
American Pie • Back in Black • Brown Eyed Girl • Landslide • Let It Be • Riptide • Summer of '69 • Take Me Home, Country Roads • Won't Get Fooled Again • You've Got a Friend • and more.
00300255 Guitar $12.99

First 50 Classical Pieces You Should Play on Guitar
This collection includes compositions by J.S. Bach, Augustin Barrios, Matteo Carcassi, Domenico Scarlatti, Fernando Sor, Francisco Tárrega, Robert de Visée, Antonio Vivaldi and many more.
00155414 Solo Guitar $14.99

First 50 Folk Songs You Should Play on Guitar
Amazing Grace • Down by the Riverside • Home on the Range • I've Been Working on the Railroad • Kumbaya • Man of Constant Sorrow • Oh! Susanna • This Little Light of Mine • When the Saints Go Marching In • The Yellow Rose of Texas • and more.
00235868 Guitar $14.99

First 50 Jazz Standards You Should Play on Guitar
All the Things You Are • Body and Soul • Don't Get Around Much Anymore • Fly Me to the Moon (In Other Words) • The Girl from Ipanema (Garota De Ipanema) • I Got Rhythm • Laura • Misty • Night and Day • Satin
00198594 Solo Guitar $14.99

First 50 Kids' Songs You Should Play on Guitar
Do-Re-Mi • Hakuna Matata • Let It Go • My Favorite Things • Puff the Magic Dragon • Take Me Out to the Ball Game • Won't You Be My Neighbor? (It's a Beautiful Day in the Neighborhood) • and more.
00300500 Guitar $14.99

First 50 Licks You Should Play on Guitar
Licks presented include the styles of legendary guitarists like Eric Clapton, Buddy Guy, Jimi Hendrix, B.B. King, Randy Rhoads, Carlos Santana, Stevie Ray Vaughan and many more.
00278875 Book/Online Audio $14.99

First 50 Riffs You Should Play on Guitar
All Right Now • Back in Black • Barracuda • Carry on Wayward Son • Crazy Train • La Grange • Layla • Seven Nation Army • Smoke on the Water • Sunday Bloody Sunday • Sunshine of Your Love • Sweet Home Alabama • Working Man • and more!
00277366 Guitar $12.99

First 50 Rock Songs You Should Play on Electric Guitar
All Along the Watchtower • Beat It • Brown Eyed Girl • Cocaine • Detroit Rock City • Hallelujah • (I Can't Get No) Satisfaction • Oh, Pretty Woman • Pride and Joy • Seven Nation Army • Should I Stay or Should I Go • Smells like Teen Spirit • Smoke on the Water • When I Come Around • You Really Got Me • and more.
00131159 Guitar $14.99

First 50 Songs You Should Fingerpick on Guitar
Annie's Song • Blackbird • The Boxer • Classical Gas • Dust in the Wind • Fire and Rain • Greensleeves • Road Trippin' • Shape of My Heart • Tears in Heaven • Time in a Bottle • Vincent (Starry Starry Night) • and more.
00149269 Solo Guitar $14.99

First 50 Songs You Should Play on 12-String Guitar
California Dreamin' • Closer to the Heart • Free Fallin' • Give a Little Bit • Hotel California • Leaving on a Jet Plane • Life by the Drop • Over the Hills and Far Away • Solsbury Hill • Space Oddity • Wish You Were Here • You Wear It Well • and more!
00287559 Guitar $14.99

First 50 Songs You Should Play on Acoustic Guitar
Against the Wind • Boulevard of Broken Dreams • Champagne Supernova • Every Rose Has Its Thorn • Fast Car • Free Fallin' • Layla • Let Her Go • Mean • One • Ring of Fire • Signs • Stairway to Heaven • Trouble • Wagon Wheel • Yellow • Yesterday • and more.
00131209 Guitar $14.99

First 50 Songs You Should Play on Bass
Blister in the Sun • I Got You (I Feel Good) • Livin' on a Prayer • Low Rider • Money • Monkey Wrench • My Generation • Roxanne • Should I Stay or Should I Go • Uptown Funk • What's Going On • With or Without You • Yellow • and more!
00149189 Bass Tab Arrangements..............$14.99

First 50 Songs You Should Play on Solo Guitar
Africa • All of Me • Blue Skies • California Dreamin' • Change the World • Crazy • Dream a Little Dream of Me • Every Breath You Take • Hallelujah • Wonderful Tonight • Yesterday • You Raise Me Up • Your Song • and more.
00288843 Guitar $14.99

First 50 Songs You Should Strum on Guitar
American Pie • Blowin' in the Wind • Daughter • Hey, Soul Sister • Home • I Will Wait • Losing My Religion • Mrs. Robinson • No Woman No Cry • Peaceful Easy Feeling • Rocky Mountain High • Sweet Caroline • Teardrops on My Guitar • Wonderful Tonight • and more.
00148996 Guitar....................................$14.99

HAL•LEONARD®

Prices, contents and availability subject to change without notice.

www.halleonard.com

0220
014